CONTENTS

		Page
	Introduction	1
I	School Health Service. Future Development	4
II	The Child Guidance Service and Maladjusted Pupils	7
III	Approved Courses for School Doctors	20
IV	Physically Handicapped Children in Ordinary Schools	24
V	Visually Handicapped Children	27
VI	Hearing Impairment	32
VII	Infectious Diseases	35
VIII	Infectious Disease and Other Hazards from Keeping Animals in Schools	39
IX	Diseases of the Skin	44
X	Health Education	48
XI	The School Dental Service	51

Appendices

A	Statistics of the School Health Service (Tables I–X)	54
B	Statistics of the School Dental Service (Tables I–V)	64
C	Handicapped pupils requiring and receiving special educational treatment	71
D	Medical and dental staffs of the Department of Education and Science	72

ACKNOWLEDGEMENT

The Chief Medical Officer wishes to thank the Chief Education Officer, Sheffield, for permission to use the photograph on the front cover.

iv

The Health of the School Child

Report of the
Chief Medical Officer of the
Department of Education and Science
for the years 1971–1972

LONDON
HER MAJESTY'S STATIONERY OFFICE
1974

ISBN 011 270301 1

REPORT OF THE CHIEF MEDICAL OFFICER
FOR 1971–1972

To the Secretary of State for Education and Science.
Madam,

INTRODUCTION

This report covering the years 1971 and 1972 will be the last in the series of biennial reports of the Chief Medical Officer. There will be a further report covering 1973 and the first 3 months of 1974 and in this Dr. Peter Henderson, formerly Senior Principal Medical Officer, will contribute a short history of the School Health Service. That report will bear another signature as this, my sixth in the series, will also be my last.

This series of reports began with the first contributed by Sir George Newman for the year 1908 and provides a record of continuous improvement in the health of the children of this country. It is not possible to say whether the great improvement in social conditions or the actual contributions of preventive medicine have played the larger part in the overall improvement. Undoubtedly the standard of nutrition has improved progressively at least since the end of the First World War and improved environmental hygiene, especially the reduction in atmospheric pollution in the last 15 years, must have made major contributions. Preventive medicine through the control of communicable disease has certainly made a more direct contribution to the reduction of morbidity and mortality in schoolchildren in the last 25 years than can be claimed for any other age group. Five principal notifiable diseases of childhood now cause less than 1 per cent of the deaths attributed to them as recently as 40 years ago. But the ordinary statistical indices of mortality and morbidity are not satisfactory measures of the state of health of children today.

We lack reliable parameters for the measurement of health in childhood as at any other age. In particular we have no reliable methods of estimating the nutritional state. The Committee on Medical Aspects of Food Policy has developed nutritional surveys which may in time give us more satisfactory methods of appraisal but little more than the preparatory phases of that work have yet been completed.

It can be said broadly that the health of schoolchildren by such measures as we have, is still improving overall but this report calls attention to a number of aspects of health with which we cannot be satisfied. In particular the problem of mental health is even less susceptible to accurate appraisal than our problems of physical health.

In 1966 the late Dr. Dorothy Llewellin gave a general account of the Child Guidance Service as she saw it then and Dr. Kingsley Whitmore has reviewed the same ground and made an attempt to analyse the path of future development in

1

Chapter II. This chapter is necessarily somewhat speculative but it makes one point which is fundamental to any progress in this field, that the multi-disciplinary teamwork built up in the School Health Service so far must be enabled to continue when the School Health Service becomes the responsibility of the Department of Health and Social Security.

The various chapters review the present position in regard to particular groups of handicaps and underline particularly the need for improvement in methods of dealing with both visual and hearing handicap. Methods for the assessment of mental handicap are changing and special training in assessment which has continued on a centralised basis for so long is now becoming decentralised and based upon university departments of child health within the regions. The growing importance of the part played by psychological service in these assessments is discussed in Chapter II, the importance of integrating educational arrangements for the physically handicapped with those of other children is discussed in Chapter IV and some successful experiments are described.

Although progress in the control of many communicable diseases has been so marked in the last 25 years, it is highly regrettable that the effective vaccine against measles has been used on such an inadequate scale that over 120,000 schoolchildren were notified as suffering from measles in the two years under review. These were avoidable and unnecessary infections. The recent increase in scabies appears to have come to an end for the time being and there was a reduction in the number of infestations recorded in 1971. However, over 260,000 schoolchildren were recorded as being verminous during 1971, a 10 per cent increase over the previous year. This may be partly due to better reporting but it is still a sad reflection on standards of cleanliness since free effective and safe methods of treatment are available and should be applied to all those affected in the household from which a pupil comes.

Broadly at the end of 13 years as Chief Medical Officer I can record that real progress has been made in the health of schoolchildren but not enough. So much has been achieved as a result of the efforts of a devoted staff, responsibility for whose work is shortly to be transferred from education to health authorities. The School Health Service began over 70 years ago because of the inadequacy of medical resources available for children at that time. Now preventive and curative facilities are available for all children under the National Health Service but they are not enough without a staff associated with the schools and devoted to securing that the best that can be done in schools to meet the difficulties of handicapped children and to promote the health of all children is done. Although health authorities will assume responsibility for providing inspection and treatment in future, there must remain a source of informed medical guidance on health matters to those concerned with the education of the children. Arrangements are to be made to secure this, but it will be the responsibility of the new health authorities and of the education authorities to make sure they have the opportunity of having their full effect. The country is fortunate in that there is a group of highly experienced doctors who have given long and expert service in this field. Their work has been too often decried by those who have not understood it. It will be as necessary in April 1974 as it was in March 1974, and the health and wellbeing of our children will suffer unless the new arrangements not only permit this service to continue but provide it with opportunities for further development; the result of the closer association with clinical services in general practice and paediatric departments that the new arrangements for administration of the National Health

2

Service will provide. There has been much concern amongst the doctors whose careers have been in this field of preventive medicine and developmental paediatrics lest the new arrangements should impede what they are trying to do. That need not happen and it should not happen.

The report on the health of the school child for the years 1969/70, discussing the prognosis in diabetes in childhood, gives a figure of expectation of life which is quite inaccurate. The original papers have been lost and it is possible that there was a typographical error. The statement that 'the average expectation of life is less than 20 years from diagnosis' relating to children diagnosed as having diabetes is certainly wrong and it would have been more accurate to say that experience in the best clinics suggest that the expectation of life of a diabetic child at age 10 under the best management is of the order of 40 years and at the Joslin Clinic in Boston was given as 73 per cent of the expectation of life in the general population at that age.

Finally I must express my thanks to my colleagues in the medical staff of the Department and to those non-medical colleagues with whom we work. In particular I express my personal gratitude to Dr. Esther Simpson and her colleagues for the report which I have the honour to introduce.

I am, Madam,

Your obedient servant,

G. E. Godber

3

CHAPTER I

SCHOOL HEALTH SERVICE.
FUTURE DEVELOPMENT

In July 1972 the Secretary of State for Education and Science, Mrs. Margaret Thatcher, gave the following answer to a question in the House of Commons: 'The Secretary of State for Wales and I attach great importance to the continuation in the future of the same close relationship as at present between child health and education; we have wished to be assured before reaching a decision about any transfer of School Health Service responsibilities to a reorganised National Health Service that collaborative arrangements could be devised which would ensure full LEA participation.

'A Working Party on Collaboration has been studying co-operation between a reorganised National Health Service and local government, and we are now satisfied that Local Education Authorities would be closely identified with the planning of Health Authorities for child health generally. We are therefore agreed that the medical and dental inspection and treatment functions of Local Education Authorities should at an appropriate time become the responsibility of the National Health Service. Local Education Authorities would have continuing responsibility for identifying and meeting special educational needs and the National Health Service would undertake to provide them with the health advice and resources they would require for these purposes and for any other of their functions.

'The Secretary of State for Social Services, the Secretary of State for Wales and I believe that it will be in the interests of child health for there to be an integrated service. To this end we propose that the professional staff concerned should be employed by a reorganised National Health Service. There would be for each area a doctor and dentist on the staff of the area health authority with the function of advising the local education authority in the same way as do the Principal School Medical Officer and the Principal School Dental Officer now.

'I understand that consideration is still being given to whether Local Education Authorities may need to retain powers to secure advice and resources in exceptional circumstances. The report from the Working Party on this and other related matters will be circulated to all the appropriate associations for comment.'

Once the decision had been taken that the National Health Service should be reorganised and unified outside local government, it became essential to work out arrangements for co-operation between a reorganised National Health Service and the local authorities. In 1971 the Department of Health and Social Security therefore set up a working party on collaboration, and a sub-committee was invited to report on the arrangements which would be necessary if a decision were subsequently taken to transfer some school health service responsibilities to the reorganised National Health Service.

The school health sub-committee considered the school health service too important to be referred to only in general terms in new legislation, and it was felt that functions should be set out specifically in terms similar to those in Section 48 of the Education Act 1944.

Section 3 of the National Health Service Reorganisation Act 1973 has since laid on the Secretary of State for Social Services the duty to make provision for medical and dental inspection and treatment of pupils at schools maintained by local education authorities. Under the Act, local education authorities retain their responsibility for the ascertainment of children requiring special education but will look to the reorganised National Health Service to provide the necessary health staff to enable the local education authority to carry out these functions. In recognition of the special needs of school medicine, a senior doctor, with appropriate experience and training, will be appointed, in agreement with the matching local education authority, by each area health authority. This doctor will have both advisory and executive responsibility for the transferred school health service and for general medical advice to the local education authority. Similar arrangements will be made for the appointment of a dentist and nursing officer. Joint consultative committees at Area Health Authority/Local Education Authority level will provide the main forum for planning and consultation.

The responsibility for the school health service will from 1 April 1974 be that of the Secretary of State for Social Services, and it seems right to end this brief introduction by quoting what Sir Keith Joseph also told the House of Commons in July 1972:

'The Secretary of State for Wales and I attach very great importance to the role of preventive health care in the health and welfare of children and we welcome the proposed transfer of the health inspection and treatment functions from the Local Education Authorities to a reorganised National Health Service which is being announced by the Secretary of State for Education and Science. We believe that to bring the general care of children's health within the National Health Service will facilitate the future development of health services for children. We look forward to receiving from the Working Party on Collaboration between the Health Service and Local Government recommendations in detail as they affect the school health service.

'It is our intention to initiate with the Secretary of State for Education and Science and in consultations with all the interests concerned a comprehensive review of all child health and school health needs.

'We recognise the importance for the future of the School Health Service of the members of the medical, dental, nursing and other professions who are now working in it, and will continue to work in it.

'I am not yet in a position to say what grading and other arrangements will be made for the medical and dental staff concerned. These are matters which will have to be discussed with the professions' representatives before final decisions can be reached. It is important that they should enjoy within the National Health Service pay and prospects at least as good as those they have at present. The way in which their contribution to the health care of school children is made may of course be influenced in the longer term by the comprehensive review of school and child health to which I have referred. Medical Staff will, however, continue in the period immediately following reorganisation carrying out the work in which they are now engaged but as members of the team of the Area Medical Officer. I am convinced that any longer term development will still provide ample opportunity for them to continue providing such services.'

Trends in the Education of Handicapped Children

As forecast in the previous issue of this report the Education (Handicapped Children) Act took effect on 1st April 1971. Since that date the balance of the special school population has been significantly altered and now more than one child in 5 is ESN(S). Local Education Authorities have been generous in staff and equipment provided and the school health service has played its part in assessing the health needs of this group of children, many of whom have multiple handicaps.

The prospects of a considerable expansion in nursery education will help handicapped children, many of whom are additionally handicapped by lack of normal living experiences. Nursery schools and classes also offer an opportunity for observation and assessment of a handicapped child away from its own home and in a group of contemporaries. As with all school placements consideration must be given as to whether the nursery school or class has the specialist facilities needed by an individual handicapped child and to ensure that the staff understand the implications of his disability.

There is now for some handicapped children a possible alternative to the hard choice between ordinary school and special school. Special classes in ordinary schools have been provided for some handicapped children, notably those with partial hearing impairment. Recommendations for admission to these special classes must be carefully thought out and the doctors concerned must be sure that children are carefully selected taking into account temperament and personality as well as their particular disability. Special equipment and necessary supporting services must also be available. Such services may include medical and psychological advice over and above that available in the school of which the special class is a part, as well as nursing and ancillary help.

CHAPTER II

THE CHILD GUIDANCE SERVICE AND MALADJUSTED PUPILS

The Facilities for Ascertainment and Treatment: Child Guidance Clinics

The responsibility for ascertaining maladjusted pupils lies with the local education authority but authorities have relied upon the child guidance clinics to identify the children and make the first move (recommendation) to secure special educational treatment. The clinics have always had the equally important function of providing or arranging therapy in whatever form they think appropriate.

The Underwood Committee,[1] reporting in 1955, made certain suggestions about the staffing of child guidance clinics and these have remained a target for the last 17 years, notwithstanding that the Committee were very clear in stating that the suggestions represented only a realistic recruitment target for 1965. The Committee recommended that the basic child guidance team should consist of 1 consultant child psychiatrist, 2 educational psychologists and 3 psychiatric social workers, and that such a team should be able to serve a school population of 45,000. Since then, the Royal Medico-Psychological Association[2] has suggested that such a team could only adequately serve a population with 35,000 school children and the Summerfield Committee[3] have recommended that one educational psychologist can only look after the needs that arise among 10,000 children.

Table I shows just how far any of these targets had been reached by 1972.

TABLE I

Staffing of child guidance clinics
(expressed in full-time equivalents to nearest whole number)

	No. of Clinics	Psychiatrists	Psychologists	PSWs
1955	211	58	144	110
1965	406	120	314	168
1972	498	163	638	438
Underwood Committee target adjusted		(193)	(386)	(579)
RMPA target		[243]	—	[729]
Summerfield Committee target		—	[850]	—

[1] Underwood report: Report of the Committee on Maladjusted Children (1955). HMSO. London.

[2] Royal Medico-Psychological Association, London. Memorandum on the Recruitment and Training of the Child Psychiatrist (1960).

[3] Summerfield Report: Psychologists in the Education Services (1968). HMSO. London.

7

By 1972 the child psychiatrists (not all of whom were of consultant grade) had still not reached the strength recommended by the Underwood Committee and numbered only two-thirds of the RMPA's estimate of need. The number of PSWs was only a little more than one-third of Underwood's target and in spite of there being as many social workers without specialised training as PSWs the total complement of social workers was only three-quarters of that recommended. The number of educational psychologists had passed the Underwood target but reached only 75 per cent of the Summerfield estimate of need.

These national figures conceal two disquieting features. The first concerns the geographical maldistribution of certain staff. Table II shows that by 1971 both in and around London the clinics had more child psychiatric staff even than the RMPA estimate of need; that in the south-east and south-west of England Underwood numbers (U see Table II) had been just about reached, and that elsewhere in the country (with the exception of Wales) the number of psychiatrists was less than half the Underwood recommendation.

TABLE II

Regional distribution of staff—31.12.70
(expressed as full-time equivalent to nearest whole number)

Regions	Psychiatrists			Social workers			Psychologists		
	Actual	U	RMPA	Actual	U	RMPA	Actual	U	S
South Eastern	23	26	33	92	104	133	109	51	116
Greater London	35	26	33	54	77	98	58	51	115
ILEA	15	9	12	48	28	37	31	19	43
South-Western	14	14	18	31	40	53	43	28	62
Wales	10	11	14	18	33	43	26	22	50
East Anglia	1	6	8	7	18	23	18	12	27
East Midlands	8	13	17	18	40	52	32	27	60
West Midlands	11	20	26	37	61	78	38	41	91
North-Western	13	27	34	50	80	102	70	53	119
Northern	6	14	17	14	41	52	39	27	61
Yorkshire & Humberside	10	19	25	30	57	74	37	38	86

The situation regarding social workers was even less favourable, since 50 per cent (60 per cent of PSWs) were working in and around London and in the South East, although only one-third of the school population live there. In ILEA the RMPA target had been passed and in the South-East and South-West of England Underwood numbers had nearly been reached but the remaining regions were, roughly speaking, only half-way towards the Underwood target.

The educational psychologists were spread much more evenly throughout the country. London and the South-East employed only 39 per cent; in all but two regions there were more psychologists than Underwood had hoped for; and whilst in the South-East there was almost one psychologist per 10,000 children, all but two of the other regions were more than half-way towards the Summerfield target.

The second feature is that the productivity of the clinics has only marginally increased (see Table III). The number of clinics has rather more than doubled in

TABLE III

Child guidance clinics: treatment rates

	School population (in millions)	No. of pupils known to have received treatment under child guidance arrangements (in thousands)	Treatment rate per hundred pupils	No. of child guidance clinics	No. of pupils treated per clinic	No. of child psychiatrists (in FTQ)	No. of child psychiatrists per clinic
1955	7·2	30·9	0·43	211	147	58	0·27
1972	8·7	74·7	0·85	498	150	163	0·32

17 years. Four per 1,000 of the school population were known to have received treatment at the clinics in 1955, whereas in 1972 the figure was 8 per 1,000. But on average the number of child psychiatrists per clinic was still only 0·3 full time equivalents and each clinic on average only catered for three more maladjusted children in 1972 than in 1955. There was also a wide variation in the case-load per psychiatrist in the different regions.

The Facilities for Special Education: the Special Schools

The progress in providing special schools for maladjusted pupils has followed a common pattern: as the number of special school places increases, so does the demand. Within the last ten years the number of establishments and their accommodation for maladjusted pupils has rather more than doubled but the waiting list for school placement has also doubled (see Table IV). Maladjusted children

TABLE IV

Educational facilities for maladjusted pupils

	1955	1962	1972
No. of Establishments (excluding hospitals)			
Residential schools	32	43	136
Day schools	3	13	61
Classes	17 (part-time)	69	141
Hostels	45	36	41
		161	379
No. of pupils in all establishments (excluding hospitals)	3,278	5,008	14,208
No. awaiting placement	681	971	1,822
Total	3,959	5,979	16,130

now form the second largest group of handicapped pupils. Maladjusted boys outnumber girls in the special schools by almost 7 to 2, although the ratio in those attending child guidance clinics is only 3 to 2. Adolescents aged 12 or over attending the schools amount to 1·2 per 1,000 pupils and the rate of attendance among primary school children is 0·6 (see Table V).

TABLE V

Age and sex of maladjusted pupils in Maintained Special Schools (1970)

	Children aged 5–11		Children aged 12–16	
	Nos.	Rate per 1000	Nos.	Rate per 1000
Boys	2,113	0·9	2,658	1·8
Girls	629	0·3	666	0·5
Total Pupils	2,742	0·6	3,324	1·2

The Demand for Child Guidance Services

There has been uncertainty about what should be regarded as a reliable assessment of the incidence of emotional instability and psychological disturbance among school children; different observers have made their assessments against different backgrounds. For example, the results from *ad hoc* studies commissioned in Birmingham, Berkshire and Somerset by the Underwood Committee in the early 1950s gave rates varying from 5·4 to 12 per cent. The lower figure was arrived at after joint consideration of children by psychiatrists and psychologists and it has generally been found that rates based upon interviews are rather lower than those based upon replies to questionnaires.

In the Isle of Wight in 1971 6·8% of 10- and 11-year-old children were regarded as having a psychiatric disorder. This study[4] depended upon an initial screening of a total age group, followed by individual interviews with child, parents and teacher. Also, the criteria used were subjective but specific: psychiatric disorder was rated as present when, considered in relation to the process of the child's psychic development, abnormalities of behaviour, emotions or relationships were sufficiently marked and sufficiently prolonged to be causing persistent suffering or handicap to the child himself, or distress or disturbance in the family or community, which was continuing up to the time of assessment.

In a national study of 7-year-old children[5] it was found that 14% had scores based upon teachers replies to questions in the Bristol Social Adjustment Guide which placed them in the maladjusted category.

It is likely that some of the differences between epidemiological studies represent community variations. Whilst there did not appear to be a strong association between social class and anti-social behaviour in the National Child Development study, the overall rate of maladjustment did show certain social class and regional differences. In the Isle of Wight social conditions were judged to be overall a little better than in the rest of England and Wales, and there was appreciably less overcrowding and there were no areas so physically unsatisfactory and liable to disintegration as in parts of some industrial centres. This could be a reason why the rate of psychiatric disorder in one such area has since been estimated as half as much again as in the Isle of Wight, adopting the same criteria.

The prevalence of a disorder is not necessarily the same as the size of the demand for services. A defect is not necessarily a disability and a disability does not necessarily constitute a handicap to growth and development of a child, his capacity to learn and to arrive at social adjustment. However, by definition the Isle of Wight children with psychiatric disorder were either handicapped or a problem to others. Their disorders called for action whether this was limited to diagnosis and advice (one-third of the cases) or probably a definite need for treatment (another one-third). Capes[6] also judged that about one in three of the 12–15-year-old children studied in her clinic required 'insight therapy'. The Underwood Committee had reckoned that no more than about 1% of the school population

[4] Rutter, M., Tizard, J., and Whitmore, K. (1970). 'Education, Health and Behaviour.' Longman, London.

[5] Davie, R., Butler, N., and Goldstein, H. (1972). 'From Birth to Seven. A Report of the National Child Development Study.' Longman, London.

[6] Capes, M., Gould, E., and Townsend, M. (1971). 'Stress in Youth.' Published for the Nuffield Provincial Hospitals Trust by Oxford University Press.

might need treatment at any one time so that the threshold is now set appreciably lower. The demand for referral to child guidance clinics depends upon a number of factors, including the behaviour-tolerance level of parents and teachers, and their attitudes to disturbed behaviour as well as their own interpretations; also it must depend upon knowledge of the existence of the child guidance service, as well as willingness to attend. Whereas half of the parents of the children with psychiatric disorder in the Isle of Wight study acknowledged that a problem existed only one in five wanted help and three out of four of the parents with children showing socialised delinquency said they positively did not want help!

The Effects of Attendance at Child Guidance Clinics

The demand for child guidance clinics also depends upon the confidence that referral will produce results. Unfortunately after 50 years of child guidance services there is still little firm, recorded data about their role and value. Shepherd and his colleagues[7] went so far as to suggest that the improvement rate among children attending a clinic was no higher than among children with similar psychological disturbances who were not attending a clinic. There would probably be general agreement that:

the problems of approximately two-thirds of the children who are referred to the clinics seem to resolve over a period of time; there is some suggestion that this is not necessarily due to intervention by the clinic but there is also some agreement that the clinics are being used for a group of children who need them;

the prognosis for the group of children with predominantly neurotic disorders is on the whole good, irrespective of treatment, though there is no way at present of recognising the child whose difficulties may persist into adult life;

the prognosis for children with an antisocial, conduct disorder may be quite good if this is a transient reaction to environmental stress but it is poor when persistent and associated with factors that stem from social and familial disorganisation. Operating over a long period, these produce developmental deprivation and personality damage.

The Demand for Special Schools

The real need for special schools for children with behaviour disorders is equally difficult to judge. The national rate in the school population of pupils attending special schools for the maladjusted in 1970 was 17·6 per 10,000 school children but it varied amongst different LEAs between 0·3 and 56 and in the different regions of England and Wales between 6·9 and 39·5.

The Effects of Special School Placement

The effects of the attendance of maladjusted pupils at special schools and classes has seldom been analysed or documented.[8] Most maladjusted children in special schools are in residential schools but whilst many of these children may need to live for much of the year away from their own homes it is not at all certain whether

---

[7] Shepherd, M., Oppenheim, B., and Mitchell, S. (1971). 'Childhood Behaviour and Mental Health.' University of London Press.

[8] Roe, M. C. (1965). 'Survey into Progress of Maladjusted Pupils.' Published by Inner London Education Authority.

the better arrangement overall, socially and developmentally as well as educationally, is to place them in residential schools, hostels or even in care. The value of hostels has seldom been documented[9] nor have their comparative costs been calculated. For a child to be taken into care as beyond parental control and then transferred three times a year to a residential special school seems the least satisfactory arrangement.

Again, the available evidence suggests that:

the children attending residential special schools include many for whom the prognosis is poor but this must to a great extent be due to the fact that these schools are particularly used for children with persistent conduct disorders (if only because they are excluded from their own schools);

the residential schools are rather selective (for a variety of reasons) but even they cannot always manage the children they admit; it is much more difficult to find a school for an adolescent than for a younger child and the rate of expulsion is higher among adolescents;

there is some evidence that residential schooling is least appropriate for adolescents and that frequent changes of schools exacerbate their behaviour disorders.

The Present Situation Summarised

From the point of view of services for maladjusted children it would seem reasonable to venture a tentative estimate that perhaps one child in ten and more boys than girls at some time during their middle school years have problems of a personally or socially disturbing kind which might benefit from help; that among the children with physical and educational handicaps the proportion will be higher than this; that all these children require interview and diagnosis but only a third of them are likely to need psychiatric intervention for advice or treatment; and that many of the remainder who have conduct disorders are unlikely to respond to either psychiatric treatment or residential school placement. It should then be noted that at present less than one child in a hundred is referred to a child guidance clinic; that at present the peak age of those so referred is 9 to 10 years but that very many of these children will have been showing evidence of their difficulties by the age of 5 years; and that if more effective help could be given to children in infants' schools and residential institutions were more selectively used the need for any more residential schools for the maladjusted might be reduced.

This is an unsatisfactory situation that calls for some fresh thinking. The matter is highly complex and two aspects only will be considered here.

Terminology and Classification

The Handicapped Pupils and Special Schools Regulations 1959 define maladjusted pupils as:

'. . . pupils who show evidence of emotional instability, or psychological disturbance and require special educational treatment in order to effect their personal, social or educational readjustment.'

---

[9] Bennett, C. (1971). 'Care for the Emotionally Disturbed Child at the Hawthorns Hostel, Cambridge.' Medical Officer, 4 June.

Like all the definitions of handicapped pupils the term refers only to those who need special education, among all children who may show emotional instability or psychological disturbance, but this is often overlooked. It is however unique among the definitions in its offer of special education as a manner of effecting something other than educational advance, i.e. social and/or personal readjustment. This has had its rewards in the form of an appreciable increase in recent years in the development of both educational and out-patient medical facilities for children with behaviour disorders but now the continued use of such an ill-defined term, which can mean all things to all people, tends to hinder progress in providing more specific services for such children.

For instance, many people, including some doctors, apply the term equally to all children with emotional and behaviour disorders irrespective of their etiology; thus, children with manifest psychiatric illness and those with organic brain disorders as well as others with developmental difficulties may all be described as maladjusted. Not only does this over-simplify the concept of maladjustment but it tends to imply more important medical (i.e. pathological) factors in all maladjusted children such as exist only in a minority. Consequently it invites a concept of treatment and cure based upon the medical model and this is not always appropriate. A good deal of disturbance in childhood is a normal psychological response to stress in which case it is not so much the child as his environment that should be judged abnormal; the absence of disturbing reactive behaviour would then be a matter of more medical concern than its presence. The failure to differentiate more precisely the specific treatment needs of individual children showing various behaviour disorders has also been the root cause of the indiscriminate school placement of many of them. It is not uncommon for some children to be ascertained as maladjusted principally in order to achieve their removal from the influence of their home, whilst for others such classification has concealed particular therapeutic and educational needs that not all schools for maladjusted pupils can necessarily provide. One consequence has been that children with all kinds of emotional and behaviour disorders, of multifarious etiology and needing all manner of different treatment and management, have tended to congregate in one kind of educational establishment—or more precisely under one kind of regime. The head teachers of some of the Inner London Education Authority's day schools for maladjusted children have been critical of the attempt to meet the needs of psychotic, brain-injured and neurotic children as well as those 'probably reacting in a healthy way to environmental factors',[10] in the same way. Another consequence has been that local education authorities have remained unaware of the true demand for certain special educational facilities.

Another aspect of this matter, although one not entirely within the hands of local education authorities or child guidance staff, has been the obligation to retain a separate classification and associated set of management options for dealing with maladjusted pupils and delinquent citizens of school age according to the manifestation of their psychological disturbance. Attention has been drawn[11] to the misconception that delinquent boys are necessarily similar to

---

[10] Day Schools for Maladjusted Children (1970): Report of a Group of Head Teachers in the Greater London Area. Pub: Assoc. of Workers for Maladjusted Children London.

[11] Mason, P. (1968): Paper read at the Cropwood Round-Table Conference 1968. In: 'The Residential Treatment of Disturbed and Delinquent Boys.' Eds. Sparks, R. F., and Hood R. G., University of Cambridge, Institute of Criminology.

maladjusted or deprived boys and that only the force of circumstances dictates whether they are placed in approved schools. There is nevertheless a good deal of overlap in the characteristics and the needs of children in approved schools and in schools for the maladjusted,[12] whilst it has also been said[11] that many of the boys in approved schools who do not have damaged personalities or psychiatric illness could equally well be treated in a variety of more general residential communities. Yet the tendency in the past has been for seriously delinquent young citizens to be dealt with on a disciplinary and punitive basis (and delinquent children from disorganised, socially under-privileged homes may have been the more likely to be so treated) and for children whose anti-social behaviour did not lead to their appearance before a juvenile court to be designated maladjusted pupils and thereby forfeit eligibility for treatment within an approved school regime.

The Children and Young Persons Act 1969 has gone a long way to overcome this anomaly for the delinquent child, since it has replaced approved school orders with orders for children to be placed in the care of local authorities and it has helped to set up a variety of institutions or Community Homes to meet the needs of children in care, designating approved schools as but one form of Community Home. However the facilities and regimes of Community Homes are only available to maladjusted pupils if they have first been taken into care. The continuation of two separate educational services, one for some of those children who live in Community Homes and another for the rest of the child population, has meant that local education authorities still need to provide a greater variety of special educational facilities within their own schools.

This underlines once again the need for child guidance clinics to be more specific in their recommendations for special educational treatment. Formal categorisation of a child as a maladjusted pupil is normally not necessary before he is offered a place in a special school; it is many years since the Secretary of State received a parent's appeal under Section 34 of the 1944 Education Act in respect of such a pupil. But even if it were necessary it should be supplemented by a description of the needs of the child and explicit advice about therapy and the sort of care that could meet those needs.

The Department is at present considering, with the help of its Advisory Committee on Handicapped Children, the possibility of dispensing with the use of defined categories of handicapped pupils, which tend to result in the labelling of children according to the nature of their disorder, and requiring instead that recommendations of a practical kind be made based upon identified educational and treatment needs. As a corollary to this, special schools could be identified by the specific nature of the services they are able to provide. If these suggestions were eventually adopted school placement for children with behaviour disorders would then be guided by advice from various child guidance staff rather than ascertainment in an omnibus class of 'the maladjusted'. There are, of course, similarities as well as differences between children in social, educational and medical institutions, and the question of homogeneous versus heterogeneous populations in

[11] Mason, P. (1968): Paper read at the Cropwood Round-Table Conference 1968. In: 'The Residential Treatment of Disturbed and Delinquent Boys.' Eds. Sparks, R. F. and Hood, R. G., University of Cambridge, Institute of Criminology.

[12] Asuni, T. (1963). Maladjustment and Delinquency: A comparison of Two Samples. *J. Child Psychol. Psychiat.* **2**, 219.

institutions can and should be answered in a variety of ways. But some form of classification of the behaviour disorders of children is necessary if appropriate facilities for their treatment is to develop in a variety of situations. Perhaps child guidance staff could experiment with the use of a triaxial classification of mental disorders in childhood which has been suggested for international trial.[13] The three axes concern:

1. the clinical psychiatric syndrome—a primary diagnosis reflecting the clinical manifestation and descriptive aspects of the disorder;
2. the child's intellectual functioning;
3. etiological or associated factors.

As well as assisting in the formulation of more precise recommendations for treatment, such a classification might also facilitate studies of the epidemiology of behaviour disorders and of the effects of treatment by child guidance staff and in special schools.

The Future Role of the Child Guidance Clinics

Theoretically, the demand for more services for children with behaviour problems could be met by more child guidance clinics. This would require more professional staff. Whilst the prospect of soon obtaining more educational psychologists and social workers might seem reasonably good it would be much less easy to increase as quickly the number of trained child psychiatrists, of whom there is at present the more serious shortage. Additional senior registrarships in child psychiatry have been established in the hospital service so that within a few years the annual output of consultants will have increased. But it is difficult to see how this will do more than keep pace with the present referral rate in a total school population that will also have increased, unless it is accompanied by a significant change in the manner in which most child guidance clinics operate.

In spite of the importance of social, cultural and educational factors in the genesis of behaviour disorders much of the practice and teaching in the clinics has continued to focus on the unravelling of psychic processes within the child and on inter-personal relationships within the family. This is immensely time-consuming and it would seem that the clinics can make little inroad into the number of children waiting to be seen or the time they have to wait for an appointment so long as every child referred is given a routine 5 to 10 (though it may be 20 to 25) hours diagnostic work-up and only one new case is seen per child psychiatrist session.

Nor should it be overlooked that this traditional approach may exclude consideration even of other medical factors that may be important. For instance, it is rare for neurological function to be assessed and clinics have in the past been very reluctant (if they have not refused) to take on the management or treatment of behaviour disorders occurring in children with epilepsy or with mental retardation.

Some clinics, it is true, have already made attempts to modify their procedures, for example by an initial sorting of referrals by the psychiatrist and selection of those for whom the full team approach is required; by shortened treatment regimes, and by crisis intervention. Others have tried working within school

---

[13] Rutter, M. *et al*. (1969). A Triaxial Classification of Mental Disorders in Childhood—An International Study. *J. Child Psychol. Psychiat*. **10**, 44.

premises.[14,15] Such experiments are to be welcomed but the fact is that the child guidance clinic service in its present form has not yet shown that it can provide the answer to the problem of how to help the majority of children with behaviour disorder: nor has it convincingly demonstrated when it has apparently successfully treated or helped some children among the minority referred, that this is an efficient and economical use of a limited amount of expertise.

More trained child guidance staff are certainly required but the greater need is for those that are available to explore new ways of helping to stem the tide of referrals and for much more use to be made of the potential skills of other personnel, beginning with the teachers.

In the first place the clinics need to be considerably more involved than at present in prevention. A WHO working party has said that '. . . what is urgently needed (for the mental health of adolescents and young persons) is re-orientation towards the preventive aspects . . .' and that this calls for '. . . a different, more flexible role for the psychiatric team, renunciation of its professional isolation, and a far more intense commitment to the community, its institutions and its problems'.[16] The child guidance service is often thought of as a preventive service and it was the dream of the pioneer clinics that they would reduce the incidence of mental disorder in children. This dream has not really come true,[17] for children only make contact with the service when a problem has arisen that their parents and/or teachers cannot manage.

In the second place it is now realised that society has probably expected too much from the psychiatrist in the cure of children with behaviour disorders. This was no doubt in the minds of the working party[18] which met to consider services for seriously disturbed adolescents; they suggested a practical grouping of adolescents according to treatment needs which distinguished between those with an illness for which medical treatment was predominantly needed and those with behaviour which was deviant from normally accepted standards for whom medical treatment was of minimal value and socio-educational treatment was all important.

It was also very much in the minds of those responsible for the Isle of Wight study.[4] They stated quite clearly that the diagnosis of psychiatric disorder did not imply that treatment would necessarily benefit the child nor that psychiatrists were necessarily the most appropriate therapists for any treatment that might be required. In fact they asserted that most children with psychiatric disorder would need to be treated by people other than psychiatrists, having particularly in mind teachers, psychologists and social workers as well as school and family doctors.

---

[14] Little, W. R., and Marshall, A. M. (1965). 'A Child Psychiatric Team visits Local Schools'. Medical Officer, 25 February.

[15] Jones, N. (1971). The Brislington Project in Bristol. *J. of Special Education*, June 1971.

[16] May, A. R., Kahn, J. H., and Cronholm, B. (1971). 'Mental Health of Adolescents and Young Persons: Report of a Technical Conference.' Public Health Papers, No. 41. WHO, Geneva.

[17] Caplan, G. (1964). Beyond the Child Guidance Clinic. Address delivered at the Twenty-fifth Anniversary celebration of the New Orleans Mental Hygiene Foundation.

[18] Interim Report of the London Boroughs Association Working Party on the Provision for Seriously disturbed Adolescents (1967).

[4] Rutter, M., Tizard, J., and Whitmore, K. (1970). 'Education, Health and Behaviour.' Longman, London.

Perhaps one of the less desirable consequences of sophisticated specialist services is that they tempt the non-specialist too readily to opt out of personal engagement in dealing with a problem himself. The clamour for more child guidance clinics should not be allowed to divert attention from the responsibilities—and the opportunities—of teachers to prevent and manage the behaviour problems of their pupils in school.

From the point of view of prevention these opportunities are greatest in the primary school[19] but it has been observed that the primary school teacher is insufficiently prepared or experienced to take advantage of this.[20] Ways and means have therefore to be found whereby school doctors and educational psychologists can lend support to teachers and advise them about attitudes and about organisation within the class and the school that promote the social and emotional adjustment of children and help alleviate the problems of those who have behaviour disorders. Child care workers in community homes need similar support and advice. As it is, psychologists spend less than a quarter of their time with children and teachers in schools[3] whilst it has been suggested that the social worker has withdrawn too much from the child's home to her own office in the clinic.

School doctors, educational psychologists and social workers have a crucial rôle to play also in giving support and treatment to individual children and their families. They require more training in child development and management if maximum use is to be made of their ability to help in this way. Child psychiatrists must be prepared to spend much more time in such post-graduate instruction in the conviction that much of what they do could be done by others if they were appropriately trained and that as specialists they should be used very much as a second line of defence, both in the hospital and in other institutions.

There is a very real need for operational research into how resources may best be deployed in providing child guidance facilities for the many children who need it; and this must be associated with clinical trials into the effectiveness of various forms of treatment. The reorganisation of the National Health Service presents an opportunity for this kind of study.

In the meantime the more obvious suggestions that have been made above are entirely consistent with the various forms of regrouping that may be discerned among the professional staff who are (or should be) contributing to the child guidance service. There is already a trend for the psychiatrists to work more closely with their colleagues in hospital—and not only the child psychiatrist but also the paediatrician and adult psychiatrist. Some regional hospital boards now enable child psychiatrists they appoint to clinics to undertake sessions in hospital and to have responsibilities (opportunities) for in-patient care. The reorganisation of the National Health Service in 1974 will result in the transfer to the area health authority of the psychiatrists, psycho-therapists and doctors in the school health service at present employed by regional hospital boards and local education authorities, and this is likely to strengthen their professional relationships with other doctors working in the health services concerned with children. The reorganisation will

[19] Webb, L. (1967). 'Children with Special Needs in the Infants' School.' Colin Smythe Limited, London.
[20] Moore, T. (1966). Difficulties of the Ordinary Child in Adjusting to Primary School. *J. Child Psychol. Psychiat.* 7, 17.
[3] Summerfield Report: Psychologists in the Education Services (1968). HMSO. London.

also see the transfer from the local education authority to the area health authority of some but not all of the premises in which child guidance clinics at present operate. There will thus be dual responsibility for providing facilities for joint clinical sessions of doctors, psychologists and social workers. It begins to look as if a new pattern of child guidance services will emerge which is less medically dominated, but is founded on collaboration between those in the basic disciplines, including general practice and paediatrics to produce a network of child guidance facilities. What this might mean in practice is that, as now, the child psychiatrist, social worker and psychologist would be employed by their respective authorities but no one authority would be administratively responsible for a child guidance service as a separate entity. It would also mean that members of each discipline would continue to work as closely together as they do now but not all the time in one setting (the child guidance clinic) and not only as an indivisible team when behaviour disorder is the principal problem. Each member would be free to engage in an appropriate rôle more independently for some of the time, and more often than at present where he normally works with children. It needs to be recognised that the school psychological services, the social service departments and the school health services each have an important part to play in their own right in the prevention and management of behaviour disorders in children, supplementing the team methods which will always be required for a proportion of the children.

Some people fear that the sharing of administrative responsibility for providing a network of facilities for child guidance will interfere with or reduce collaboration between the professional staff of the health, education and social service authorities but they should not forget the long tradition of multi-disciplinary co-operation among the key child guidance personnel and arrangements for joint sessional work can quite easily be part of any contract of employment.

As health centres continue to be used as a focus for the development of community health services and include facilities for child guidance, the direct involvement of the primary care team in dealing with behaviour disorders in children will become easier. It is particularly important that doctors and nurses doing child welfare and school health work and paediatricians also, should be in close touch with child psychiatrists, educational psychologists and social workers if they too are to play a more active part. The Underwood Committee regarded the school doctor as an essential member of the child guidance team; in practice this is still the exception but there is urgent need for it to be the rule.

CHAPTER III

APPROVED COURSES FOR SCHOOL DOCTORS

It is essential that children be fully investigated before decisions are made regarding their special education, whether or not special school placement is likely to be recommended. Such investigation should normally be arranged quite informally. The fact that formal ascertainment is not necessary before a local education authority can offer, and the parents accept, a place for a child in a special school (see DES Circular 11/61[1]), has sometimes been interpreted as meaning that a medical examination is not necessary either. The reason for this no doubt has been that formal ascertainment as set out in Section 34 of the Education Act 1944 includes a medical examination. However, good clinical practice dictates that a medical examination should form part of any investigation of a child who may need special education, however formally or informally it may be arranged.

In the case of children likely to need special education as educationally sub-normal pupils there are regulations governing the qualifications and experience required of the doctors who conduct the medical examination. This is the only instance in which the Secretary of State has exercised the power conferred by Section 69 of the 1944 Education Act to prescribe special qualifications and experience for examining medical officers.

The Medical Examination (Subnormal Children) Regulations, 1959, require that unless he has been approved under the School Health Service and Handi-capped Pupils Regulations 1953 or he is a psychiatrist working in a child guidance clinic, a doctor who is employed by an authority to examine children who may be mentally or educationally subnormal must first have attended a special, approved university post-graduate course of instruction and also have assisted in such examinations carried out by a duly qualified medical officer. On receipt of a certi-ficate of satisfactory attendance at one of these courses and after spending a proba-tionary period of six months assisting, the doctor is recognised as qualified to examine such children for any local education authority.

The Regulations issued in 1959 will lapse when the National Health Service Reorganisation Act 1973 becomes operative in April 1974 but it is intended that similar regulations will be made governing the qualifications expected of doctors who examine subnormal children.

The approved courses available to school doctors over the last ten years were described in the report on the Health of the School Child for 1960 and 1961, which also contained observations about the selection of doctors for this training and the six months' probation.

In April 1971, the doctors, psychologists and a few others who had been con-cerned with the organisation of these courses in the Universities of London,

---

[1] Special Educational Treatment for Educationally Subnormal Pupils.

Bristol, Leeds and Newcastle were invited to the Department of Education and Science to discuss the content and methods of the courses and to consider what changes might be appropriate. It has to be remembered that the school doctor's present rôle in the ascertainment of educationally subnormal children stems from the medical responsibility for the certification of mentally deficient persons, under the Mental Deficiency Act 1913. The 1921 Education Act later directed that children '. . . not being imbecile and not being merely dull and backward . . .' should be provided for in special classes and schools; thus it was necessary first that they be certified as feeble-minded and this was something a school doctor had to do. The 1921 Act was superseded by the 1944 Education Act but this still required a medical officer to advise the education authority which children suffered from a disability of mind of such a nature and extent as to render them unsuitable for education in school or were in need of special education as educationally subnormal pupils. Since the first course for certifying medical officers was set up jointly by the Central Association for the care of the Mentally Defective and the University of London in 1920, the emphasis in the training has consistently been upon the diagnosis of mental deficiency (now termed mental subnormality) and for the last 35 years especially upon instruction and practice in the administration of the Stanford-Binet Scale of Intelligence as an aid to diagnosis. Many modifications in the course syllabus have been made during this time, particularly in recent years in the London Course and towards the inclusion of sessions on child development and psychology. Nevertheless, in 1969, between one-third and one-half of the total number of sessions on each course were devoted to intelligence testing.

In the meantime, changes had been taking place in the services concerned with special education and in the attitudes of professional staff contributing to these. In the first place, psychology has found a place alongside medicine in the field of special educational treatment. By 1971, all but nine local education authorities were employing educational psychologists and many authorities had well-developed school psychological services; the equivalent of 555 full-time educational psychologists were working for education authorities. Secondly, the pattern of inter-disciplinary cooperation so firmly established in child guidance clinics was beginning to be discerned in the assessment of children with physical disorders and learning difficulties. School doctors and psychologists have been working more closely together in arriving at decisions and recommendations about the special education of ESN children. These trends have resulted in a more rational and economical use of the expertise of doctors and psychologists and less need for school doctors to undertake the intelligence tests.

Thirdly, there has been general recognition, not least among psychologists themselves, that there is need for considerable care and discretion in assessing the significance of an Intelligence Quotient as now ascertained. A statement of a child's IQ is of limited practical value to the teacher of a backward child compared with the help that can be derived from a detailed psychological report; this a school doctor is not qualified to give, notwithstanding that he is recognised as competent to administer an intelligence test. Since the publication of Ministry of Education Pamphlet Number 5[2] in 1946 there has been a distinct move away from dependence upon the IQ as the principal criterion for advising special school placement for an ESN child. Fourthly, the repeal of Section 57 of the 1944

---

[2] Special Educational Treatment.

Education Act consequent upon the passing of the Education Act 1970, has meant that school doctors are no longer required to advise their authorities which children are so mentally handicapped as to be unsuitable for education in school. These events have provided the opportunity for the doctor's rôle in the ascertainment of ESN children to be modified to the extent that he can concentrate on the medical aspects of the diagnosis and special educational treatment. The demonstration that the study of mental subnormality and educational subnormality is best undertaken as part of a study of child development and mental health in childhood has pointed to the need for courses of instruction for school doctors in the examination of ESN children to be more broadly based on normal child development and knowledge of neurological and psychiatric disorders in children.

It was considerations such as these that led those attending the meeting in 1971 to agree unanimously that courses of training should provide instruction and practice in the neuro-developmental and paediatric assessment of the child from a young age against a background syllabus of child development and learning, the paediatric and psychological care of children with physical and sensory handicaps as well as with mental and learning disorders, and their special educational treatment. They considered that such courses should be provided by university departments of child health but fully appreciated that staffs of other university departments and school health services would need to contribute. They did not think that the courses should attempt to achieve competence in intelligence testing by the doctors but recognised the need for the latter to be aware of the objective and methods of psychometry and the respective rôles of psychologist and doctor in inter-disciplinary assessment and that this required the active participation of psychologists, particularly educational psychologists, in the course. Finally, they expressed the opinion that such courses should be attended by all doctors who were engaged extensively in clinical work in the school health service.

Significant changes in the approved courses began to appear in 1972. The University Departments of Child Health at Newcastle, Bristol and Leeds were the first to assume responsibility for organising the new courses in collaboration with experienced doctors working in adjacent school health services. All three courses were organised on a one-day-per-week release basis, extending over two or three academic terms, although the Leeds course has started each term with a single 5-day block period covering the first week. This has limited attendance to school doctors working in surrounding authorities but it was intended that the new courses should be planned for regional rather than national use. The number of doctors on each course (from 12 to 20) has represented a compromise between enough to make the course financially viable from fees and a group small enough to allow adequate tutorial and practical experience for each doctor.

The general aim of all three courses has been to expose the doctors to current knowledge about development in normal and handicapped children as a basis for experience in the diagnosis, assessment and, to some extent, treatment of children with various physical, sensory and mental disorders that interfere with development and learning; one specific intention has been that the doctors should acquire an expertise in the examination of children with learning difficulties that is not dependent upon the administration of the Stanford-Binet test of intelligence. The most convenient and effective course pattern for achieving these objectives will probably take a little time to evolve.

Similar day release courses were scheduled in the University Departments of Child Health at Birmingham and Liverpool for early in 1973, and plans are well advanced for courses in Sheffield and Cardiff later in the same year.

The courses in London, arranged jointly since 1947 by the Extra-Mural Department of the University and the National Association for Mental Health, have always been the principal source of this training for school doctors. For the last decade or so, approximately 80 doctors have attended each year; Bristol, Leeds and Newcastle have together provided on average another 40 places. The last of the traditional courses will take place in London in the autumn of 1973. It is anticipated that within a year or two the establishment of alternative regional day release courses will go a long way towards filling the gap in national facilities for training that would otherwise appear after in 1974. However, similar training courses will still be needed by doctors working in school health services in London and the home counties and these are now being discussed with the University's Departments of Child Health.

CHAPTER IV

PHYSICALLY HANDICAPPED CHILDREN IN ORDINARY SCHOOLS

In Circulars 85/70[1] and 13/70[2] of August 1970, which relate to the Chronically Sick and Disabled Persons Act 1970, it was suggested that 'many less severely handicapped can be satisfactorily educated in ordinary schools and benefit from mixing with the general run of their contemporaries'. This supplemented the advice given previously (Circular No. 276 25 June 1954) by the Department that 'no handicapped pupil should be sent to a special school who can be satisfactorily educated in an ordinary school'. Efforts are being made to ensure that at least one ordinary school in every area is suitable for physically handicapped pupils, in accordance with the spirit of the 1970 Act.

Whilst accepting these general principles there remain some physically handicapped children for whom a special school provides the most satisfactory placement, albeit with the chance to transfer to an ordinary school when, as the result of a comprehensive review, this is felt to be advisable on medical, educational or psychological grounds. There are still some misgivings about the wisdom of attempting to integrate into ordinary schools those children with severe physical handicaps which prevent them from mixing readily with normal children. However, where conditions have been made suitable and the teachers have accepted the challenge, there have been some notable successes particularly among the children with severe congenital limb deformities. Several of these children have severe reduction deformities of all four limbs, as well as other physical defects, but the severity of their disability has been of less importance than the commonsense approach of the teachers and acceptance by the other children and their parents of a severely physically handicapped child in their midst, together with the sensible use of special aids and adaptations to the school furniture.

On the other hand, examples have been seen of physically handicapped children failing to receive the necessary supporting medical, nursing, physiotherapy, psychological or speech therapy services when an Authority has pursued, perhaps too enthusiastically, a policy of 'integration' of most of its physically handicapped children. Even with the provision of a welfare assistant or classroom helper it would seem doubtful if the numbers of children in the classroom of the ordinary school allowed the teacher to devote sufficient time to the majority of pupils or to provide the elements of special education needed by the handicapped children. It may indeed by necessary to limit the number of physically handicapped children in any one school or class.

---

[1] Joint Circular from the Welsh Office and Department of Education and Science.
[2] Joint Circular from the Department of Health and Social Security and Department of Education and Science.

In the survey of physically handicapped children in ordinary schools previously reported[3] 128 children considered to need physiotherapy and 122 children considered to need speech therapy were not receiving it. Because of the shortage of therapists these services are more easily provided for a small number of special schools than for the very large number of ordinary schools. Sending children to a therapist at a hospital is expensive in terms of transport and time lost to education; it might be possible to consider the use of a peripatetic physiotherapy service or of children receiving their physiotherapy out of school hours.

There is no longer any justification for attaching a label, or category, to a child and automatically sending him to a special school. Alternatively, it would be dangerous to decree that all physically handicapped children could attend even suitably adapted ordinary schools. Some children can accept it and some are psychologically, socially, medically or educationally unable to do so.

Teachers who are going to work successfully with physically handicapped children may need to overcome some of their own personal feelings, they may find great difficulty—as many people do—in close association with the seriously ill child with, for example, leukaemia or cancer, or the child whose condition is deteriorating from muscular dystrophy and who is doomed to die and may be aware of this. The school doctor should be able and willing to help such a teacher to overcome his or her feeling of inadequacy in such a situation as well as to explain how a particular disability may be expected to affect the child's ability to learn. If a teacher is to be encouraged to notice signs and symptoms indicating that a physically handicapped child is not well and may need urgent medical attention for a blocked intra-cranial valve, urinary affection or failing kidney function, she must, with the parents' knowledge, be given the relevant facts of the child's medical history in intelligible form and in discussion either with the school doctor or nurse or the family doctor as well as by the written word. This provision of a professional team to support the physically handicapped child requires much effort and thought to be successful. The ability to work harmoniously in a professional relationship with colleagues of different disciplines has to be learned and implies a mutual respect as well as a willingness to compromise. The Medical Adviser to the local education authority and his staff have an important rôle to play in the school and should be able to be regarded as a friend, ready and willing to discuss problems as well as to take part in the periodic review of the children's progress. It is manifestly necessary that this rôle should be fulfilled in agreement with the family doctor who has the oversight of treatment.

The acceptance of a child wearing a prosthesis in the classroom may initially evoke curiosity and questions from the other children and the teacher may be given help and reassurance by the occupational therapist or physiotherapist as well as practical help with the management of the apparatus. It has been said that the more visible the disease, or disability, the greater are the problems involved. Children with an atrio-ventricular shunt for the treatment of hydrocephalus association with myelomeningocele may be expected to have a different set of difficulties from those of the child with hydrocephalus alone and either may have some educational retardation.

The relationship between the class teacher and the child is very important during these formative years. Everything possible needs to be done to ensure that

[3] Report of the Chief Medical Officer of the Department of Education and Science 1969–70. HMSO.

it is on a sound footing and free from any feeling of hostility, sentimentality, or an over-protection of the handicapped child which could lead to a failure to ensure that he works as hard as he is able and derives as much benefit from his education as possible. The handicapped child has special need of the full benefit of education so that he may take his rightful place in life after school and measure up to the demands placed upon him by society while accepting the limitations imposed upon him by his handicap.

Physically handicapped children who are not placed in an ordinary school may be admitted to a class or unit attached to the ordinary school where they are enabled to receive the special help they require as well as sharing the life and activities of the school as a whole. It is important, however, to ensure that this results in integration in the school group and not segregation of the handicapped child.

A group of 12 children with severe limb deformities whose parents were anxious that they should be educated in ordinary schools was admitted to a unit in an infants school in a city in the North East of England in the Spring of 1968. At first the children were taught in the two classrooms which formed the unit and which had specially adapted toilet accommodation but after the first two days they joined the full school assembly and after the first month they ceased to have their midday dinner in their own classrooms and they played with the normal children of their own age groups. They were quickly able to be absorbed into the several classes of the school according to their age and ability. This integration was brought about spontaneously and happily and the children took part in the normal school day, arriving at about 8.50 a.m. and leaving at 4 p.m. In the initial stages the headmistress had the support of teachers with experience of limb deficient children and an occupational therapist, a welfare assistant was appointed to help with the children's toilet requirements.

In another city in the North Midlands, while a survey was being carried out to ascertain what structural alterations and staffing might be needed in ordinary schools to accommodate handicapped children, it was found that 333 physically handicapped children were already integrated into their nursery, primary and comprehensive schools, although this local education authority had also several special schools for the physically handicapped. An on-going evaluation of this provision for handicapped children has been proposed by this local education authority. Physically handicapped children may also be admitted to the special schools on the same sites as ordinary schools, sharing the facilities between the schools, or to special schools from which they may undertake part of their studies in local ordinary schools or colleges of further education.

Independence of any kind is most important to a disabled person and the special school may enable a child to learn to be independent in a controlled environment and with more privacy than in a large class at an ordinary school. The smaller teaching ratio now suggested should benefit children who have to miss school for hospital treatment, such as those with myelomeningocele who may need periodic attention to their valves as well as other operative treatment. Flexibility in school placement and regular review of the child's progress should however ensure that the physically handicapped child is placed in an educational environment which is from all points of view in the child's best interests. This flexibility is most easily secured when special units and special schools are closely linked with ordinary schools.

CHAPTER V

VISUALLY HANDICAPPED CHILDREN

Strabismus and variations in visual acuity continued to be the most frequent conditions recorded at medical inspections of schoolchildren. During 1971, out of a total school population of 8·5 million, 3 million pupils were examined at periodic, reinspection or special medical examinations: of these 130,849 schoolchildren required treatment, and a further 240,920 observation, for variations in eyesight: 22,417 pupils were treated, and 21,135 required observation for squint. Over 380,000 schoolchildren were examined and treated by school medical officers or consultant ophthalmologists in either the local education authority or hospital medical services; of these over 187,000 had spectacles prescribed.

Vision Screening in School

During 1971, 155 (95·1%) local education authorities in England and Wales screened pupils for variations in eyesight within the first year of entry to school: Nine authorities delayed vision screening by one or more years, four of these until the child was 6 years of age and five until the pupil was 7 years old. This is an improvement on 1966 when sixteen authorities did not screen entrants to school, but there is no evident reason why all authorities should not do so for school entrants. Delay in screening means delay in the correction of some visual defects; during this period these infant schoolchildren may be at a disadvantage in their general educational progress.

The Committee of Enquiry into the Education of Visually Handicapped Children in its recent report recommends that vision screening of all schoolchildren, including annual tests of visual acuity, should be part of the School Health Service in all primary and secondary schools and special schools for other handicaps. Such annual reviews of schoolchildren, between the ages of 5 and 16 years, were, in fact, achieved by nineteen authorities (11·6%); another four authorities (2·4%) provide annual vision screening but omit one or two years at either end of the age range; thirteen authorities (8%) operate a biennial programme of vision screening. Many authorities tend to concentrate their vision screening programmes on certain age groups such as 5 year-old entrants, 7 or 8-year junior entrants, 10 or 11 year-old junior leavers and 14 or 15 year-old school leavers: screening for visual defects may, at these ages, be associated with routine medical inspections. In the annual returns submitted by Principal School Medical Officers, it is evident that pupils aged 6, 9, 12, 13 and 16 years in many authorities do not have their vision tested: e.g. less than one authority in four screens 6 year-old pupils, and one authority in three screens 12 year-old schoolchildren for visual defects. Twenty-one authorities (12·8%) provide vision screening tests from one to three times during the whole period of their pupils' school career; forty-seven (28·6%) screened the vision of their schoolchildren 4 times during the 5–16-year age range. Thus two out of five authorities provide vision screening programmes from one to four times during the whole 12-year period a child is in school. Many of these sixty-eight authorities review children with known defect of vision annually, and also keep under annual surveillance pupils with suspected defective vision. One local education authority, however, in 1971, did no routine vision screening after the age of 5 years, and another nine authorities omitted routine vision screening of children in secondary schools. There are considerable gaps in time, ranging from 4 to 6 years, between subsequent retests, in the services provided by some authorities, although most of these authorities review children with a known visual problem annually or biennially. Where programmes for screening vision are deficient, children who may require treatment are being denied this, in some cases for considerable periods of time; these children are put at a disadvantage in their education.

Colour Vision

Colour vision testing using Ishihara test plates or vision screening machines was performed by 159 authorities; five authorities in England and Wales do not test for colour vision: twenty-seven authorities retest children, this being done in the first instance in primary school and repeated towards the end of the pupil's secondary-school career. The age of testing varied from 5–15 years: 107 (67·3%) of the 159 authorities testing for colour vision defect do so between 9 and 11 years of age; thirty-three authorities (20·7%) elect to test for colour vision defect at 14 or 15 years. Boys only were tested for colour vision defect by 40 LEAs, although many of these will test girls at discretion of the school medical officer or in response to a request from the parent or teacher.

A new instrument, for detecting colour vision defects quantitatively and qualitatively, has been developed by Dain (Community Medicine, 26.8.72, p. 149). This apparatus operates on the principle of using a complete hue circle of 26 permanent glass filters which can be presented in any degree of saturation. These are matched with a central achromatic colour filter; those with normal colour vision are said to be able to identify the only matching pair within 2 minutes: the use of a darkened room is required for testing. Detailed colour vision testing of children found to be defective in colour vision may take 15–20 minutes. This apparatus known as the Lovibond Colour Vision Analyser is already in use in some hospitals.

Bacon (Medical Officer: 16.4.71) in a Survey of Hampshire schoolchildren postulated that colour vision defect is an educational handicap. He found in seeking evidence of teaching situations in which schoolchildren with defective colour vision might be at a disadvantage, that teaching staff recorded an impressive array of such situations. A series of prepared tests given to schoolchildren throughout the school age range showed that some but not all colour vision defective children confused colours under the test conditions, and in discriminating between colours at entrance age, normal children confused closely similar material, while the children with defective colour vision showed greater confusion in discrimination. Marginally significant retardation in arithmetic was noted in 13 year-old boys with colour vision defect; the survey suggested that there were fewer children with colour vision defect in ESN schools. The evidence provided by this survey is considered sufficiently firm to justify routine screening of colour vision early in school life for both boys and girls.

28

Personnel Engaged in Vision Screening

The staff involved in vision screening, either alone or in combination, includes school medical officers, health visitors, school and clinic nurses, nursing auxiliaries, audiometricians, and trained assistants such as clerks, education welfare officers and screening machine operators. Two authorities use orthoptists and one small authority a qualified optician. School health departments still rely very heavily on school nursing staff in carrying out routine vision screening; 150 authorities (91%) indicate that nursing staff are mainly responsible for vision testing. Screening for colour vision testing, apart from a small number of authorities using ancillary personnel, is undertaken almost equally by school medical officers or nursing staff. There appears to be no consistent pattern in the use of vision screening machines throughout the country: a few areas use these in infants schools but in the main they are used to screen junior- and secondary-age pupils. Children failing a vision test are, in most areas, reviewed by the school medical officer or health visitor to reduce unnecessary reference to ophthalmologists. Regular vision screening performed by trained staff is important to the health of schoolchildren.

Committee of Enquiry into the Education of Visually Handicapped Children (The Education of the Visually Handicapped: HMSO)

This committee was appointed in October 1968 to consider the organisation of education services for the blind and partially sighted and to make recommendations: the members of the committee, who had as their chairman Professor M. D. Vernon, had a wide variety of background and experience. They included teachers of normal and visually handicapped schoolchildren, lecturers in teacher training colleges and universities, doctors, psychologists and administrators in local education and health services; in addition two parents of handicapped children served on the committee. Two members (as well as one of the assessors) were themselves blind. The committee presented its report in November 1972.

In their summary of recommendations, the committee consider that the total number of places required over the next decade for visually handicapped pupils in special schools should be assumed as approximately the same as at present; they recommend that a national plan for the reorganisation of the educational services for the visually handicapped should be implemented and for this purpose committees should be set up on a regional basis to prepare plans for short and long term needs. The requirements of pre-school children with visual handicap are recognised as being in need of particular attention; and the committee stress the necessity of regular assessment in these visually handicapped young children and in children of school age, by opthalmologists, paediatricians (and other consultants where indicated), school medical officers and school nurses, from the medical aspect, and by specialist teachers and psychologists from the educational aspect. Support and counselling for parents, in particular for those with children under 5 years of age, should be made readily available. Pre-school visually handicapped children should have access to a range of educational facilities in each area, and at some stage should receive some form of education. Annual vision screening of all children in all primary and secondary schools and special schools for other handicaps is advised, and where visually handicapped pupils attend normal or special schools for other handicaps the ophthalmic services provided for these children must be of the standard pertaining in schools for the visually handicapped.

Recommendations on the medical surveillance of visually handicapped pupils include more frequent general medical examinations than in sighted children, regular visiting of schools for the visually handicapped by ophthalmologists and opticians, close links with child guidance and child psychiatric services, and genetic counselling for parents and older pupils. Local education authorities are urged to make their school medical and dental services available to all children in day and residential schools for the visually handicapped.

Discussing the organisation of schools for the visually handicapped, the committee recommended that all blind and partially sighted children, except some with multiple handicap or poor home conditions, should live at home if their home is within one hour's journey from a suitable school with the proviso that the parents can be given guidance on child management. Where day school attendance is impracticable, weekly boarding is preferred to continuous boarding; local education authorities are urged to help with travelling home at weekends. The committee have reviewed various methods of educating blind and partially sighted children at different stages of their school career, as well as further education, higher education, vocational guidance, and training of teachers and residential child care staff. They suggest that systematic experiments be carried out within a national plan in the education of visually handicapped pupils in ordinary schools either in ordinary classes or special classes. Child care staff working with visually handicapped children should have relevant qualifications and more in-service training in child management should be provided.

The report highlights the diverse needs and special requirements of the visually handicapped child and his family; these can only be met by a multi-disciplinary approach involving medicine, education, psychology and social work, combining in a team to extend to visually handicapped children further opportunities in their education and adult life.

Visually Handicapped Pupils With Other Handicaps

There are thirty-nine schools in England and Wales which provide education for visually handicapped pupils (eighteen blind, nineteen partially sighted and two catering for both defects); in addition there are eighteen special classes or units in ordinary schools or special schools for other handicap. Included in this total are six Sunshine Home schools, one primary and one secondary school admitting blind children with other handicaps. In addition to these, there are units for children with defects of hearing and vision attached to some special or ordinary schools, and in one hospital. Borocourt Hospital has a small unit for primary age children who are maladjusted and blind mainly for assessment and short term education; two hospitals at Bromsgrove and at Reigate have special units for mentally subnormal blind children.

In January 1972, there were 1,232 blind and 2,422 partially sighted children receiving education in special schools, independent schools, special classes or units, residential homes and hospitals or were awaiting admission to special school, giving a national incidence of 1·49 blind and 2·92 partially sighted per 100,000 schoolchildren. An, as yet, unknown number of visually handicapped children were transferred to the education services in April 1971 when responsibility for the education of mentally subnormal children was vested in the local education authority. In a survey in the North Midlands Region, a medical officer of the Department found that of 2,313 children in day schools for severely mentally handicapped children, 81 (3·5%) were known to have a significant visual handicap, and of these 36 were blind; many of these 81 children, in addition to their mental and visual defects had associated physical and social handicaps. This survey was limited to day school pupils, and did not include children living at home or resident in hospital.

School medical officers and teachers dealing with visually handicapped children have become aware of the increasing identification of multiple handicap among these children in recent years. A survey carried out in 1969, by a member of the Committee of Enquiry referred to above, noted that of a total of 1,916 pupils in partially sighted schools, classes and units, 449 suffered from an added handicap which was in itself sufficient to require special educational treatment, and a further 423 had less severe defects which created educational problems in conjunction with their partial sightedness. Physical handicap and educational subnormality were the two most commonly found additional handicaps in visually handicapped children; maladjustment, epilepsy, speech and hearing defects were recorded frequently. Not enough is known about the effect of other major handicaps in visually handicapped children, and further investigation is needed in this field to provide for the special educational requirements of these multiply handicapped children.

CHAPTER VI

HEARING IMPAIRMENT

Screening for Hearing

The principle that defects of hearing should be diagnosed as early as possible either after birth, in the case of congenital deafness, or following an injury or illness which could cause acquired deafness, is well established. The means by which this principle is applied include routine screening for hearing of both pre-school and school children. The sources of information on the services provided by Local Health Authorities and Local Education Authorities include the Annual Reports of Medical Officers of Health and Principal School Medical Officers, surveys such as that carried out by DHSS in 1969, and the annual return made by Local Education Authorities to the Department of Education and Science on Form 8M(iv).

Taking the information from Form 8M(iv) 1971 as a starting point, Local Education Authorities can be divided by the audiometric services they provide under the School Health Service into 6 groups as follows:

1. Those who have no facility for audiometry.
2. Those who arrange audiometry for school children only when it is individually requested, i.e. only when children are 'referred'.
3. Those who arrange routine audiometry on all entrants during their first year at school which, for the purposes of this report, is taken to be at the statutory age of 5 years.
4. Those who arrange the first routine audiometry during a child's second year at school, i.e. at the age of 6.
5. Those who arrange the first routine audiometry during a child's third year at school, i.e. at the age of 7.
6. Those who arrange the first routine audiometry during a child's fourth year at school, i.e. at the age of 8.

Returns for 1971 were made by 145 Local Education Authorities, one making no return. (It should be stated that the Inner London Education Authority made a single return on behalf of the thirteen Inner London Boroughs which have therefore been counted as a single Authority for this purpose.)

Group 1

Five Local Education Authorities, one County, four County Boroughs and nearly half of another county, fall into the first group, though two of the County Boroughs do not use pure tone audiometry but arrange tests, one by 'forced whisper', and the other by spoken word lists.

Group 2

Eight Local Education Authorities arrange audiometry only on referral, or for selected groups of school children such as those known to be handicapped, or to

32

be at risk of hearing impairment. Four Counties and four County Boroughs adopt this practice and at least some of them accept referrals from a wide range of sources, e.g. from parents, teachers, School Medical Officers, school nurses and speech therapists.

Groups 3 and 4

127 Local Education Authorities carry out routine screening of all school children during their first or second years at school, i.e. at the ages of 5 or 6, ninety-five doing it during the first year at school, thirty-two during the second year.

Group 5

Three Local Education Authorities, all County Boroughs, fall into this group.

Group 6

Two Local Education Authorities, one County and one County Borough do their first routine test on school children aged 8, i.e. during their fourth year at school.

It is desirable that all school children should have their hearing tested as soon as possible after they enter school, unless it has been done shortly before entry under a system of pre-school medical examination. The service provided by Local Education Authorities in groups 1, 2, 5 and 6 most need further examination. Services provided by the Local Health Authorities corresponding to the Local Education Authorities in these groups for pre-school and particularly children under the age of 12 months, must be taken into account. In 1969 DHSS conducted a survey and asked Local Health Authorities the following questions, among others as follows:

1. Have you a scheme for the routine screening of infants between 6 and 12 months? Yes/No
2. (a) Is an attempt made to screen ALL infants? Yes/No
2. (b) If 'Yes' are you satisfied that coverage is virtually complete? Yes/No
3. If only a proportion of infants are screened, what groups are selected?
   Clinic attenders
   'At-Risk' Register
   Handicap Register
   Other (state ....)

A report on this survey was included in the Annual Report 'On the State of Public Health' 1969, pages 108 to 109, and can be summarised as follows:

'Replies were received from 157 Local Health Authorities. 138 Local Health Authorities had a scheme for routine screening of infants aged between 6 and 12 months (question 1), 97 such Authorities made an attempt to screen all infants (question 2(a)), but in only 45 of them was coverage virtually complete (question 2(b)). 42 Authorities attempted to screen only selected groups (question 3), some including, as well as the 3 groups on the questionnaire, children referred by, for example, doctors, nurses, teachers or parents and those with speech defects.'

Of the eighteen Authorities without schemes for routine screening on school entry, ten do not screen the hearing of all infants, but all but one of them screen one or more selected groups of infants. Five of these ten Authorities screen the named groups. In some instances, where less than the recommended level of audiometry is provided for school children there has been fairly substantial coverage of 6- to 12-month-old infants sufficient to detect most of the children with congenital hearing defects. Hearing impairment, particularly that of lesser degree, acquired in later childhood or early school life would not be detected as early as is desirable, and of course the screening methods used in infancy are necessarily less certain than those available at later ages. In terms of coverage of the child population approximately 60% of school children have their hearing screened routinely during their first year at school, and another 26% have it screened during their second year at school. Routine audiometry is not provided for 7·8% of school children (i.e. no audiometry or audiometry on referral only: groups 1 and 2) and a further 4·5% of school children do not have their hearing tested routinely until they have been at school for more than 2 years.

Both the questionnaires, the DHSS 1969 Survey and the DES Form 8M(iv) provide information on who performed the hearing tests. In nearly every Local Health Authority it was the Health Visitor who did the initial screening for hearing in babies. In the School Health Service in 1971 there were 11 categories of staff engaged on 'audiometry', some Authorities using staff in more than one category. Much the greater part of this work is apparently carried out by 2 groups of staff, firstly by School Nurses, Health Visitors and Clinic Nurses, and, secondly, by non-professional staff given titles such as audiometricians, screening assistants, audiometry assistants, hearing assessment officers. Much of the training in screening techniques is thought to have been by in-service methods, though some at least of the nursing staff have attended more extensive training courses. The other categories of staff include audiologists, School Medical Officers and teachers of the deaf though it seems unlikely that many of them are in fact engaged on routine audiometry. Clearly the major part is played by nurses, that is health visitors and school nurses, and it is manifestly important that, in planning future services, their need for training in detection of hearing impairment in both pre-school and school children should be fully recognised.

CHAPTER VII

INFECTIOUS DISEASES

In 1971 slightly under 87,000 schoolchildren aged 5–14 years were recorded by the Registrar General as suffering from notifiable disease, and in 1972 less than 84,000 notifications were recorded: these figures are slightly more than half those received for 1970. Measles, scarlet fever, infective jaundice, dysentery and food poisoning remain the most frequently notified infectious diseases among schoolchildren. Measles, accounting for over two-thirds of the total notifications, continues to be the most commonly recorded infection in schoolchildren aged 5–14 years, and as formerly the majority (over 70%) of these are in the 5–9-year age range: 59,831 notifications in the 5–14-year age group were received in 1971 and 66,201 in 1972. The introduction of measles vaccine in 1968 has contributed to the considerable reduction in the numbers of schoolchildren suffering from this disease; serious adverse reactions to the vaccine are very few especially after the age of 2 years. Follow-up investigation of children immunised against measles has shown that they were still immune to measles infection after 7 years (Miller: Community Medicine: 22.9.72). If immunisation against measles were more widely accepted there could be a much more substantial reduction in the prevalence of this disease. The problem of measles immunisation is, however, more complex than with other immunisations. In the past, practically all children in our society have contracted the disease, and if epidemic occurrence is to be prevented it is specially important to protect all children by immunisation. The reduction in the numbers of children aged 5–14 suffering from scarlet fever has continued: 8,173 notifications were recorded in 1971 and 7,119 in 1972. Whooping cough has continued to be less prevalent among schoolchildren with 7,021 notifications in 1971 and a very considerable reduction to 688 in 1972: the reduction in 1972 is thought to be due to the improved protection given by vaccines now available. Adverse reactions may follow pertussis vaccination, and this should not be given where there is a history of convulsions nor should further doses of the vaccine be given if the child has a reaction to the first dose of the vaccine (Jamieson: BMJ: 27.1.73).

Among the 5–14 age group there were 7 cases of diphtheria notified in 1971, and 1 in 1972. The Principal School Medical Officer for Manchester in his annual report describes an outbreak of diphtheria which occurred in February 1971, in which there were 8 cases of this disease: 4 of these 8 patients had not been immunised and another child had only had a primary course 9 years previously, and one pre-school child who had not been immunised died. Investigation of this outbreak revealed among adults and children 28 carriers of virulent organisms and a further 22 carriers of non-virulent organisms. Immunisation was at first offered to all children under the age of 16 in the locality of two schools involved and 6,500 children were immunised: this was followed by a campaign to immunise pre-school and schoolchildren in the city. A total of 75,000 (70,000 schoolchildren and 5,000 below school age) were immunised, and of these 14,000 had never previously been immunised against the disease (Community Medicine: 22.9.72).

35

Diphtheria is a lethal disease and so long as a significant proportion of parents remain indifferent to the protection against diphtheria provided by immunisation, outbreaks such as occurred in Manchester will continue. In some areas the percentage of children in the community immunised against diphtheria is high, but in others the percentage figure is distressingly low: for example, of children born in 1969 and immunised by 31 December 1971 there were areas with percentage figures below 50. Tetanus was notified in 5 children of school age in 1971 and in 2 schoolchildren in 1972: one of these was a 13 year-old Indian boy who had not previously been immunised and who developed tetanus after a head injury; the organisms were recovered from a middle-ear infection. Otogenic infections of tetanus are reported to occur in as many as 20% of cases in India (*BMJ*: 6.1.73). Prophylaxis against tetanus should be offered to all children and this point should be remembered in Indian children with a history of aural disease. Poliomyelitis was notified in 3 schoolchildren in 1971 and in 2 in 1972: 4 of these children developed residual paralysis. Diphtheria, tetanus and poliomyelitis are preventable diseases: the price of neglect or indifference in not ensuring a high level of immunity among schoolchildren will be the continuing occurrence of sporadic cases of these diseases.

The teratogenic effects of rubella infection in the foetus is well established and the aim of rubella vaccination is to protect the foetus from such an infection. In this country vaccination is provided for all girls between their 11th and 14th birthdays so that those susceptible to rubella will be protected against this disease before reaching child-bearing age. There is no evidence that the vaccine virus is teratogenic but susceptible adult women are not encouraged to be immunised against rubella unless precautions against pregnancy within 8 weeks of being vaccinated are strictly followed. In addition to more frequently reported congenital defects Forrest and Menser report 9 cases (20%) of diabetes and latent diabetes in 44 young adults with a history of congenital rubella (*Lancet*: 14.8.71), and Feldman *et al.* suggest that congenital rubella should be considered as a possible aetiology in some language disorders (*Lancet*: 30.10.71). It has been thought unlikely that rubella can be eradicated by immunisation and it is therefore important to ensure that susceptible girls are immunised: there is evidence to suggest that suitable levels are not everywhere attained. Acceptance rates for rubella immunisation among schoolgirls in this country range from below 50% to above 90%: for example, in one LEA only 2,500 girls were vaccinated against rubella out of a total of 11,000 schoolgirls eligible under the scheme.

Acute meningitis and acute encephalitis were reported in 647 children of school age in 1971 as against 435 children in the previous year; in 1972, 531 children were notified as suffering from these diseases. Outbreaks of Echovirus type 4 meningitis/encephalitis have been reported from Belfast and Teesside: these both began in the last quarter of 1970 and continued through the first half of 1971. In both outbreaks the peak incidence was among schoolchildren, with 32 cases in the 5–14-year age range in a total of 56 in the Belfast outbreak, and 33 cases in a total of 77 in Teesside (PHLS: CDR 71/25). The clinical signs and symptoms included headache, nausea, vomiting, neck stiffness, photophobia, and occasionally a macular rash: recovery was rapid after an illness lasting 48 to 72 hours. Infection with *Neisseria meningitidis* is the most frequent cause of bacterial meningitis and an outbreak was reported in 1971 from a school involving three 13 year-old schoolboys. There has been an increase in prevalence of this disease in Western Europe in recent years and Britain has shared in this misfortune.

36

In the period 1971–72 there has been a decline of notifiable diseases affecting the alimentary tract in schoolchildren aged 5–14 years. Infective jaundice is most frequently notified with 6,416 reported in 1971 and 5,276 in 1972; the numbers notified in 1972 are less than half those in 1970. Dysentery was notified in 2,868 schoolchildren in 1971 and 2,281 in 1972, while cases of food poisoning in this age group were 1,066 and 869 for 1971 and 1972 respectively. In this period, reported notifications of typhoid fever among children aged 5–14 were 35 (1971) and 29 (1972): these figures being very similar to the two previous years. Paratyphoid fever in schoolchildren declined from 65 notifications in 1970 to 21 in 1971 and 15 in 1972: the majority of typhoid and paratyphoid infections are imported from abroad. Outbreaks involving schoolchildren and staff in schools of food poisoning and dysentery continues to be reported although the overall incidence has been declining in recent years. In one such outbreak in 1971, 40 children in an infant school became ill with gastro-intestinal symptoms, caused by infection with *Shigella sonnei*: the disease quickly spread to involve four schools and home contacts. A health education campaign lasting 5 days was instituted in which twenty-three schools were visited and circulars giving advice on personal hygiene and prevention of spread of the disease were distributed to 5,300 children to give to their parents, and posters and leaflets were distributed throughout these schools. In addition health education publicity material was distributed to other professional, commercial and industrial bodies and to the local press. An outbreak of Sonne dysentery occurred in March 1971 in a London borough following a school cruise to the Middle East, in which *Shigella sonnei* was isolated from 64 children out of a total of 595 pupils who went on this cruise. Ice cream purchased ashore may have been the infected vehicle.

Thompson, Hutchison and Johnston, in a survey of intestinal pathogens in immigrant children (*BMJ*: 4.3.72), screened 4,000 immigrant schoolchildren in Birmingham for intestinal helminths. Of these 4,000, 37% showed evidence of helminthic infections; the rates were highest among children from the West Indies (51%) and lowest in children from Kenya (16%) and Uganda (7%): children from the Indian sub-continent had carriage rates for worms of between 30 and 40%. More than one type of worm was recorded in 36% of those affected; 5 children had concomitant salmonella infections of which two were due to *Salmonella typhi* which responded to treatment. Eradication of helminths may be difficult particularly where more than one type of helminth is involved and also because of difficulties of communication with some immigrant families. These authors suggested that immigrant children newly arrived in this country might be screened for helminths, both for their own protection and that of others. Trials with new single-dose anti-helminthics have been shown to produce over 90% cure rates against roundworm, hookworm and threadworm infections (*Arch. Dis. Childhood*: June 1972).

Respiratory tuberculosis among children aged 5–14 increased marginally in 1971 when 631 notifications were received, but decreased to 614 in 1972. Tuberculosis of the central nervous system and meninges increased to 27 notifications in 1971, but fell to 15 in 1972: other forms of tuberculosis accounted for 177 notifications in 1971 and 162 in 1972. BCG vaccination against tuberculosis is provided through the school health service between the ages of 10 and 13, and over half a million pupils were vaccinated in England and Wales in 1971. This number is still well short of the desired levels. The Department of Health and Social Security, Scottish Home and Health Department and Welsh Office have issued a Medical

Memorandum (Memo 322/BCG (Revised 1972)) advising on PPD, tuberculin testing techniques, dried BCG vaccine, groups to be vaccinated, vaccination technique, complications, record keeping and ordering of supplies. The memorandum recommends that immigrant children coming from communities in which there is a high incidence of tuberculosis should be regarded as contacts, and suggests that since Heaf Grade 1 reactions in children are not usually related to infection with *Mycobacterium tuberculosis*, schoolchildren with Heaf Grade 1 reactions should be offered BCG vaccination.

In July 1971 the Secretary of State for the Social Services accepted the recommendation of the Joint Committee on Vaccination and Immunisation that smallpox vaccination need not be recommended as a routine procedure. This advice was based on the reduced prevalence of smallpox in countries abroad and the diminishing likelihood of the occurrence of outbreaks in this country. However, travellers to or from countries in which smallpox is endemic, or countries where eradication programmes against smallpox are in operation, should be protected by recent vaccination. Malaria was recorded in 21 schoolchildren in 1971, compared to 11 such notifications in 1970. There was an increase in 1972 when 58 children were notified as suffering from this disease; the existence of malaria should be kept in mind in immigrant children and in those travelling from endemic malarial areas.

CHAPTER VIII

INFECTIOUS DISEASE AND OTHER HAZARDS FROM KEEPING ANIMALS IN SCHOOLS

In recent years increased interest in the study of man's environment has been a feature of many schools. In studying the environment, schoolchildren learn how plants and animals exist, their interaction with each other, and how man himself is affected by changing circumstances within his environment. In many schools, subjects such as biology, nature study and rural/environmental studies are included in the curriculum, but rarely however is attention drawn to the potential hazards for man, from animals acting as reservoirs of infection. The habit of keeping animals as pets is widespread in this country: in many homes, the animal is frequently considered to have almost the same status as a member of the family, and similarly in schools, they are often regarded by schoolchildren as much loved members of the school community. To a large extent, familiarity in keeping animals as pets at home and in school, may lead to neglect of their potential as vectors of disease, and of hazards which may be associated with them.

Animals in schools are commonly seen in nursery, primary and special schools. In secondary schools they are most frequently associated with biology or rural/environmental departments, and often a variety of different animals are kept within the school buildings or grounds of residential schools. A surprising diversity of animals are maintained in schools ranging from invertebrate creatures to herbivore farm animals; these animals can be sources of great interest, study and activity for pupils in school.

Range of Animals Kept in Schools

A wide range of invertebrate animals are commonly kept by schools. These include indigenous creatures such as worms, snails, woodlice, caterpillars (foreign species, particularly tropical silk moths are now quite common) and a variety of pond insects. Stick insects are also popular, particularly in primary schools. Bee-keeping is an interest which is sometimes fostered in both primary and secondary schools. Micro-organisms such as Amoeba, Colpidium, Paramecium, Hydra and Artemia are most likely to be found in secondary schools, while Drosophila, cockroaches and locusts are popular subjects for study at more advanced levels.

Tropical and cold-water aquaria are popular features in many schools as are small cage birds such as budgerigars, canaries and foreign finches. Occasionally larger birds such as parrots, parakeets, mynahs, macaws, quail, pigeons, pheasants and bantams are also seen in schools.

Amphibia, mainly frogs, toads and newts are often raised from tadpoles. Xenopus or the African clawed toad has become very popular with the advent of Nuffield Science and green tree frogs and salamanders are quite popular examples of foreign amphibians found in schools. A variety of reptiles are also sometimes housed in vivaria: these may include common lizards, slow worms and sometimes grass snakes. Of the more exotic reptiles tortoises and terrapins are the most popular although young iguana lizards (often sold as green lizards) and even baby alligators are not unknown. There are many factors apart from disease risk (e.g. safety, conservation and often cruelty implicit in this trade in foreign material) which give grounds for discouraging the keeping of these in school.

Small mammals such as mice, rats, gerbils, hamsters, guinea pigs and rabbits are among the most popular animals seen in classrooms. Sometimes British wild mammals are also found in schools, and these may include hedgehogs, voles and occasionally foxes and badgers. Cats and dogs sometimes become attached to classrooms as pets. Poultry, most frequently hens, and less commonly ducks, geese and turkeys are the most common representatives of farm livestock, but the larger herbivores such as sheep, goats, horses, cattle, and pigs are not uncommon in secondary schools with established rural studies departments. Very rarely species of primates have been seen in schools.

The sources from which these animals come into school may vary: the children or a member of the staff may introduce the animal into school; in other instances the animal may be a stray animal adopted by the pupils, or it may be purchased from a dealer. With the rapid travel facilities now available, the importation of animals from abroad may increase the risk of transmission of disease as the animal may be a silent carrier of disease, or may not develop symptoms of an infection until after arrival in this country. It is often not fully realised that animals may harbour organisms capable of transmitting infection, nor the extent to which animal related diseases may affect the health of children who are those most often in intimate contact with these animals.

Animal Related Infections

Zoonoses or animal related diseases are widespread throughout the world: infection may be mild in the animal but may produce severe symptoms in man (e.g. brucellosis); or an infection may be severe in the animal but mild if contracted by man (e.g. Newcastle disease); or infection may be equally severe in both man and animal (e.g. rabies). The stringent control by quarantine of susceptible animals, the precautions taken by port health authorities, and the regulations issued governing the importation of animal products, reflect the seriousness with which animal related diseases are regarded. Animals can be infected by bacteria or viruses, and carry fleas or other parasites capable of transmitting infection; they can also be infested with worms or fungi. Salmonella infections are common in many animals; birds such as canaries, budgerigars, hens, ducks and parrots may suffer from salmonellosis; rodents and rabbits are known to have produced this infection in adults and children handling the animal. Terrapins are also known to carry these organisms in their gut; a recent report from the Public Health Laboratory Service (Communicable Diseases Report 19.5.72) noted infection by Salmonella organisms originating from a terrapin in a 9-year-old child: follow-up investigation yielded 6 cases of enteritis and 5 excretors of these organisms, and the organisms were also recovered from 7 tank water specimens.

Many of these animals are kept in nursery, infant and special schools where the pupils are often immature and have little knowledge of hygiene; it is important, therefore, to ensure that children in school should be trained in handwashing after handling animals or cleaning out cages. Streptococcal, staphylococcal or pasteurella infections may be transmitted by bites, stings or scratches from an animal. Tuberculosis may be contracted from animals, but this is nowadays relatively rare, because of the successful programme for eradication of bovine tuberculosis in cattle; it should be remembered however, that both strains of Mycobacteria may infect animals and these, because of their close contact, may in turn infect an adult or child. Ornithosis (Psittacosis) is a disease of birds (often psittacine birds such as parrots and budgerigars): adults are mostly affected, but 3 children contracted this condition in 1971. In birds, the disease may present as a mild transient infection, or they may be healthy carriers of the disease; pigeons may be carriers of the disease, and for this reason free-flying pigeons are not permitted in schools by some Authorities. In other instances the birds may die of an acute attack of the disease. Leptospirosis is a relatively uncommon condition in children of school age, and is often spread by rodents; rats, voles and fieldmice being natural hosts of the causative organisms; pigs and dogs may also be infected with leptospira: 2 schoolchildren were reported in 1971 as suffering from this disease. Lymphocytic choriomeningitis affects guineas pigs, mice and dogs; this virus infection which is often mild in the animal, may be severe in man. Newcastle disease which affects caged birds and poultry is a virus infection to which man is susceptible, producing conjunctivitis. Cat scratch fever may produce lymphadenopathy which may then proceed to abscess formation. Primates (monkeys) are rarely kept in schools; monkeys can be dangerous sources of infections, including a B virus infection which is mild in the animal but causes a high mortality rate in man ('Keeping Animals in School': DES: 1971).

Fleas, lice, mites and ticks harboured by animals, as well as acting as vectors of specific disease, may produce skin lesions from their bites: these may range from localised transient irritation to a severe reaction in a sensitized individual. Worms are often excreted by animals and the larval stages of some worms are capable of causing disease in the human. Cats, dogs and their young, for example, are commonly infested with adult toxocara (nematode) worms; the eggs of these worms, when excreted by the animal, may be transmitted to children by handling or fondling the animal. The eggs are then swallowed and the larvae penetrate the wall of the intestine and may produce a generalised infection, affecting the retina in particular. Fungus infections are common in many animals; Bisseru (Bisseru: 'Diseases of Man Contracted from His Pets': 1967) considers that a large proportion of skin lesions due to fungal infections are contracted from animal hosts. Ringworm (over 1,000 cases of which disease were reported in 1971 in schoolchildren) can be transmitted by animals such as cats, dogs, guinea pigs, horses or cattle; in man, animal infections by ringworm are often of the pustular variety.

Allergic reactions from animal allergens occur in sensitized children, producing in most cases, wheeziness, conjunctival suffusion, rhinitis and skin irritation or rashes, of varying degrees of severity. Cats, dogs, horses and birds are known among others to be implicated in producing allergic reactions in susceptible persons. The reaction may occasionally be very severe, as occurred in a 9-year-old child in a primary school in 1972; this child, who came into contact with a rabbit in another classroom in the school, had such a marked reaction that emergency treatment from a doctor was required. The saliva of animals may contain allergens, and allergic reactions affecting the face have been reported following licking by the animal (Bisseru). A number of cases of allergy to locusts have been reported from schools keeping these insects particularly where they are kept in situations in which laboratory staff or pupils are working for much of the day ('Keeping Animals in School': DES: 1971).

The diseases mentioned in this section are by no means exhaustive of the list of animal related diseases: while some of these are rare, others such as ringworm and enteritis from salmonella infections are more common. School medical staffs, teachers and children should be aware of the potential dangers which might occur from handling animals or cleaning their cages. Personal hygiene is important, and children should be taught to wash their hands after fondling or caring for animals. Kissing of animals by children should be discouraged. Food meant for human consumption should be kept away from the vicinity of animals.

Other Hazards

Biting, kicking or scratching are natural reflex actions in many animals when startled or threatened: some animals (e.g. female hamsters) may become very aggressive when pregnant or nursing their young, and are at this time dangerous to handle. Some children may tease an animal which then responds by biting or scratching. Other children when trying to touch the animal put their fingers through the wire mesh of the cage; the animal may react by biting the child's fingers. Bites from animals are often transient injuries, but may in young children produce a temporary state of fright; bites may however become septic and may be slow in healing. Similarly scratching usually causes slight injuries which heal readily; occasionally they may become infected. Some animals may defend themselves by kicking; rabbits can kick very strongly with their hind legs, and can also produce quite severe scratching with their claws. Bee stings may occur in children in schools which have beehives; handling of bees should only be carried out under the supervision of the teacher and when protective clothing is worn. Some children may have developed a fear of a specific animal, and this may in some instances amount to almost phobic proportions; this, when present in a child, requires patient understanding, and encouragement from the teaching staff to help the child to overcome his difficulty.

Young children particularly are inquisitive and immature, and allowance for this should be made when animals are kept in the classroom. Cages and tanks should be securely fastened so that they cannot be overturned by children. Sharp edges and poorly finished cages should be avoided; projecting nails and broken wire should be covered as these may cause abrasions; glass or pottery feeding dishes are best avoided as they may break and injure child or animal: cuts or abrasions from these sources are dangerous as they may become infected.

Precautions

Scrupulous hygiene in the handling of animals by schoolchildren must be insisted on after every contact with the animal; this should consist of washing the hands with preferably a germicidal soap if this is available. Unnecessary handling of animals should be avoided, and in the case of young children, animals should only be handled under the supervision of the teacher. Children who have cuts, abrasions or open sores should avoid handling animals until the lesions are completely healed: children with known allergy to animals should also avoid contact with these animals. Hugging and kissing of animals should be discouraged. Superficial bites and scratches should be washed with soap and water and an antiseptic dressing applied. More serious lesions should be referred to a doctor with information regarding the biting animal, as antibiotic cover or anti-tetanus prophylaxis may be indicated. Where an animal is ill, it should be isolated for the welfare of both the animal and the child, and the animal should be seen by a veterinary surgeon to determine the nature of the illness.

Pet shops may sometimes offer for sale small exotic animals such as squirrels; the keeping of these should be discouraged by schools because of the difficulty of providing adequate cages and increased risk of disease. For similar reasons the keeping of indigenous wild mammals should also be discouraged. Cages and tanks containing animals should be maintained in good repair, and should be as escape-proof as possible; they should be sited in the classroom in a position which avoids their being accidentally upset by children moving around in the class, and should have a stable and secure base. Hygiene of the living quarters of the animal is important, and tanks and cages should be regularly cleaned after which the hands of the person cleaning the cage should be washed. Animal foodstuffs should be kept in secure lidded containers to avoid contamination by wild rodents and domestic dogs and cats. Initial stocks of animals should be bought from accredited sources lists of which can be obtained from the Laboratory Animals Centre, Medical Research Centre, Woodmansterne Road, Carshalton, Surrey.

In the opening comments in this chapter reference was made to the part that animals can play in the classroom: it is not the intention to discourage the keeping of animals in school, but to point out the potential risks attached to having close contacts with these animals. Careless or thoughtless maintenance of animals is unacceptable; sensible precautions in the care of animals in school will prevent unnecessary suffering to animal and schoolchild alike.

CHAPTER IX

DISEASES OF THE SKIN

The presence of skin disease is one of the most common findings at medical inspections of schoolchildren. Verminous infestation was recorded in over a quarter of a million pupils in 1971, and a further slight increase was noted in 1972: impetigo, ringworm or scabies was recorded in 25,570 schoolchildren in 1971 and in 20,595 in 1972. Other skin diseases, such as verrucae, acne vulgaris, ichthyosis, psoriasis and dermatitis were reported in 132,574 schoolchildren in 1971 and in 135,598 in 1972.

Impetigo, Ringworm and Scabies

There was a marked decrease noted in 1969 and 1970 in the prevalence of impetigo among schoolchildren and during 1971 and 1972 this decrease has continued but at a slower rate. The school health service treated 8,496 schoolchildren in 1971, and 7,374 in 1972 for impetigo, as compared with 8,568 schoolchildren in 1970. While this reduction in the numbers of schoolchildren contracting impetigo is welcome, the number of pupils affected by this condition remains unacceptably high. The increase in the numbers of schoolchildren reported by Principal School Medical Officers with ringworm infections of the body and scalp noted since 1965, was reversed during the period under review. In 1970, a peak of 1,475 ringworm infections of body and scalp was recorded; in comparison in 1971, there were 1,017 such infections, of which 679 were body infections and 338 infections of the scalp: in 1972, there were 840 cases of which 510 were body and 330 scalp infections. In 1971, while there was an increase of 95 ringworm infections of the body, there was a marked decrease of 553 infections of the scalp: the prevalence of ringworm of both types continued to decrease in schoolchildren in 1972. Since 1965, an increased prevalence of scabies occurring among schoolchildren has been reported by school medical officers; a four-fold increase in this condition was recorded in the period 1965–70 in schoolchildren. The numbers of pupils recorded as having scabies decreased from 18,857 in 1970 to 16,057 in 1971 and to 12,381 in 1972. While it is gratifying to report the decreased prevalence of these conditions in schoolchildren, these diseases occur more frequently than is necessary. There is continuing need for sustained vigilance by medical and nursing staffs in schools so that these diseases may be discovered quickly. Early, prompt and effective treatment will prevent the spread of these infections to other pupils in the school but family and other contacts of an infected schoolchild should be examined, and treated if found to be affected, since spread of infections in families is likely.

Verminous Conditions

Infestation with vermin is a preventable condition, and it is disappointing that so many of our schoolchildren are still infested. The increase in numbers of pupils reported since 1969 as found to be verminous, continued during the period 1971–

44

72. Principal School Medical Officers reported that 260,758 schoolchildren were recorded in 1971 as being verminous; 266,602 pupils were found to be verminous in 1972: in comparison, the numbers of verminous children recorded in school in 1970 was 237,813. In 1971 and 1972 slightly over 55,000 cleansing notices were issued as compared to slightly over 41,000 in 1970. Cleansing orders issued in 1970 totalled 7,280; in 1971 the total number of such orders was 5,129 and in 1972 cleansing orders were issued in 5,910 cases. Verminous conditions have received a great deal of attention over the past few years, and the increase reported in 1971–72 may, in part, be the result of more complete reporting by school medical and nursing staffs. Ignorance of the cause and spread of verminous infestation would appear to be widespread among parents and older schoolchildren, and this lack of information tends to perpetuate the continued existence of the condition among the school population. Because of this lack of knowledge, several authorities have mounted special campaigns to disseminate information on the prevention and treatment of head lice by distributing leaflets to parents, and by using local news media such as press and radio. These efforts to stimulate public concern and co-operation have been effective. One Midland authority reported a reduction of 80% in head infestation among its pupils after a campaign which began with local press coverage on verminous conditions in schoolchildren in the area. This was followed by distribution of pamphlets to parents pointing out the need for cleanliness and giving advice on prevention and treatment; school nurses and cleansing assistants made regular visits to schools to conduct inspections and to give talks and demonstrations to children on the subject of head lice.

Verminous infestation occurring in schoolchildren, like scabies, commonly reflects or soon becomes a household infestation and in many recurring cases, pupils have been re-infested from family contacts. These families need especial care from the school nurse and her cleansing assistant to persuade the family as a whole to accept treatment. Verminous infestation is a community problem, not solely a school problem; to reduce the prevalence of infestation, the community as a whole must be prepared to deal with verminous conditions within it. The school medical officer and school nurse play a major rôle in community health education against pediculosis: their determination and persistence in encouraging the necessary personal hygiene in schoolchildren and their families, together with active treatment of those found to be infested with vermin, can reduce the reservoir of infestation if a community effort is made. Pediculosis is eradicable by quite simple means.

An obstacle to the eradication of head lice has been the development of strains resistant to the insecticides which were previously effective. Because of this many authorities are now using a Malathion preparation in treatment of children found to be verminous. Malathion used in the strength required (0·5%) presents no risk to the patient in the treatment of pediculosis, but there may be a greater risk of toxic absorption in personnel handling the material repeatedly: for this reason, nurses and cleansing assistants, cleansing large numbers of children, should wear rubber gloves while using the preparation. In a survey in Northern Ireland Maguire and McNally (*Community Medicine*: 4.8.72) found that the treatment of 106 verminous children with Malathion (0·5%) resulted in an immediate success rate of 100% in boys and 89·6% in girls. In this survey more than one-third of these children were found to have one or more members of their families similarly affected. The majority of these children had been verminous for more than 6 months despite previous treatment. Maunder (*Community*

45

Medicine: 3.9.71) reported a survey in the north of England in which nearly 3,000 people were treated by Malathion (0·5%); no live lice were found on inspection 24 hours after treatment, and no side effects were noted. Malathion has a residual effect persisting for several weeks, and an ovicidal effect which prevents the nits from maturing.

Plantar Warts

Plantar Warts in schoolchildren are endemic but may from time to time reach epidemic proportions in localised areas. They are often troublesome because of the discomfort they cause the sufferer, and may limit the pupil in some school activities. Plantar warts present complex epidemiological and virological problems: they are caused by wart virus infection, the virus being a member of the papova group of viruses. The wart virion is icosahedral and has a pH in the same range as sweat (3·5–7). The incubation period is thought to be in the range of 1 to 6 months. Sufferers from this infection are liable to be unaware of it until such time as symptoms appear, by which time the infection may be well entrenched. The most frequent reasons for seeking treatment are discomfort, tenderness, pain or alteration in the normal gait. An untreated pupil with plantar wart may easily spread the infection to other children by shedding live virus. The condition is more commonly found in pupils of secondary school age and is a frequent infection seen in foot inspections and routine medical examinations.

Bunney, in an investigation of students attending a College of Physical Education, concluded that the spread of plantar warts within the student community occurred principally in the swimming pool: she suggests that the abrasive action of non-slip surfaces in swimming baths on the softened horny surface of the wart is responsible for the high rate of transmission of wart virus infections. The investigation showed that protective footwear (Plastsok) worn while using the swimming pool was effective in preventing spread of plantar warts (*Community Medicine*: 10.3.72).

Some plantar warts may disappear spontaneously, but the majority require treatment. Treatment is directed at excising or extirpating the wart, and this may be done by a variety of methods; surgical excision, curettage, diathermy, freezing or application of keratolytic agents to dissolve the horny surface layer may be used either singly or in combination. Treatment may be provided by the general practitioner, private chiropodist, hospital or local authority health services. Many local authorities have chiropody services but in the main these are naturally devoted to treatment of the elderly and the handicapped. Denvir (*Community Medicine*: 1.10.70) reviewing 10 years' experience of a School Foot Health Service in Stirlingshire comments that over 94% of patients attending local health authority chiropody clinics in 1968 were retired persons.

In 1971, 31 authorities reported that they employed chiropodists in their school health services. The Principal School Medical Officer for Holland County Council in his annual report for that year recorded that 65 children were treated by the chiropodist and a total of 291 attendances were made; all these children were treated for plantar warts. The Principal School Medical Officer for Buckinghamshire in his report for 1971 commenting on the school chiropody service, describes three basic functions performed by the service, treatment of acute conditions (e.g. plantar warts, fungus infections), prevention of potentially disabling foot conditions, and foot health education. Of sixty-eight secondary schools in the county, fifty-two were visited on a weekly basis, as were seven special schools: primary schools were visited at the request of the teaching staff or school medical officer as staffing was insufficient for regular inspection in these schools. In a pilot survey of two primary schools, the need for chiropody services has become apparent even for entrants to school. In a school population of 109,279, 10,919 treatments were given: approximately 9,500 of these were for plantar warts.

Many school medical officers and school nurses have acquired expertise in treating plantar warts in minor ailment or school clinics. Prompt treatment enables pupils to return to school activities with a minimal loss of valuable educational time. The risk of contracting infection is dependant on the prevalence of plantar warts in a community, and the regular inspection of the feet of school-children is the first line of defence in prevention of spread of the disease: by this means, affected pupils will be discovered and treated as soon as possible. Many authorities include inspection of the soles of the feet in the regular hygiene of schoolchildren. Where a school medical officer is notified that there are children with plantar warts in school, it is advisable to conduct an inspection of all children in the school and refer those affected for treatment.

CHAPTER X

HEALTH EDUCATION

Health education is an integral part of schooling. Teachers in infant, junior and secondary schools contribute to a child's understanding of health even if they are not always following any set programme of health education. This is happening throughout school life; from the beginning when the reception class teacher ensures that toilet and washing habits are understood, to the end when the sixth-form pupils may discuss the health hazards of nuclear radiation. The differing policies of local education authorities give a wide variation in the curricular content and quality of health education found in schools, but these policies do not prevent individual schools from carrying out their own well-planned programmes.

Centrally, the Schools Council and the Health Education Council are together instituting curriculum development. Locally, an increasing number of local education authority working parties are being set up to advise teachers. More teachers are attending Department of Education and Science short courses, and local education authority in-service courses on health education. All this is helping to improve the liaison between teachers, school doctors and health education officers. There are also clear signs in some university departments of education and colleges of education of a revived interest in health education and in some of these establishments students have been offered 'Health Education' as an optional part of their course. One university is seeking to establish a chair in the subject.

The normal principles of teaching apply in health education as in other subjects. The use of visiting speakers does not mean that these principles can be disregarded, however distinguished these speakers may be in their own professional fields. A teacher should always be involved so that, when appropriate, the method of introduction, discussion and open-ended project can be used, and the technical content of the visitor's lecture related to the rest of the educational programme. The responsibility for the health education programme of a school is that of the headteacher or a delegated assistant. There should be co-operation between members of staff, thus giving a co-ordinated approach that does not neglect to use as many opportunities as possible in the curriculum for promoting health education, and yet prevents unnecessary duplication. There are many 'aids' to health education in the form of films, film strips, audio tapes and books. Care should be taken that 'aids' are suited to a child's age, and mental and emotional development; it must be remembered that they are not a substitute for the teacher. Children in special schools and classes are at least equally in need of an adequate health education programme adjusted to their particular needs and level of appreciation.

Amongst the social hazards facing adolescents three aspects of human behaviour, smoking, the use and abuse of drugs, including alcohol, and sex have been of particular concern to teachers although it must be emphasised that these topics are only part of a health education programme. There must be very few local education authorities who, over the last ten years, have not organised a cam-

48

paign for schools to inform children of the dangers of smoking, thus hoping they would not acquire the habit. There is now some evidence that the proportion of smokers among young males is no longer increasing, and that among young females, after several years of rapid increase in the proportion smoking, the same levelling off may be occurring. In 1972 the Department of Education and Science issued an Education Information booklet entitled 'Smoking and Health in Schools' to help teachers understand the problem. The booklet was notable in its follow-up of the scientific review of the smoking problem both in medical and behavioural terms, with a section devoted to the wide variety of education approaches available to interested teachers.

The extent to which drug-taking occurs among schoolchildren is extremely difficult to determine. School doctors and nurses as well as teachers are aware that children could be experimenting with drugs and are watchful, yet extremely few children are discovered taking drugs on school premises. Again, to help teachers the Department of Education and Science issued in 1972 an Education Information booklet on 'Drugs and the Schools'.

Current thought is against imparting sex knowledge as an isolated subject in schools, but in favour of including such teaching in a programme that also deals with the related problems of self-awareness and human relationships that are important components of the same problems. Care should be taken that the content of such a programme is related to the appropriate stage of the child's mental, physical and educational development. This, however, is not an argument against the teaching of the principles of human reproduction in biology lessons. In our present society it cannot be wise for children to leave school without some knowledge of family planning, of the dangers of sexually-transmitted diseases and the problems of the unmarried mother and her child.

Interest is now being taken in what further health education could be given in schools that might prevent premature death or long periods of sickness in both children and adults. Mortality tables show that accidents cause the highest number of deaths in schoolchildren. More deaths occur from accidents in and around the home than in traffic accidents, but to different age groups. Most authorities, with the help of the police, teach road safety, but relatively less attention is given to warning children about hazards in the home.

In adults the death rate from heart and lung disease is far higher than from any other cause. Children are taught that smoking is responsible for some of these deaths but more should also be said about the other causes such as obesity, malnutrition (as against under-nutrition) and the over-indulgence in alcohol.

On leaving school many boys and girls will be employed in industry. They should clearly know something about the hazards of working life, the dangers of accidents at work and the care that has to be taken in certain occupations because of the risk of industrial disease. A life completely free from hazard is not attainable, or even desirable, but awareness of the risks in different modes of life at least offers an opportunity for prevention. Towards the end of school life up-to-date information on the availability of health and social services should be given and both boys and girls given an opportunity to discuss family responsibilities and child-care. Taking a still wider view older pupils should be taught more about the health problems of the society they live in. They should know more about the problems of the physically and mentally handicapped, the difficulties of the aged, and the causes of both mental and physical illness.

Teachers and many other adults are, not surprisingly, worried about the increase in drug experimentation, in pregnancy and abortion in schoolgirls, in venereal disease and violence. These trends have high-lighted the need for and importance of pastoral care in school. It is hoped that children are being helped to be more considerate of the feeling and needs of others and of their own mental and physical health.

Many problems facing young people leaving school are created or contributed to by contemporary society and too much should not be expected of the schools. Adult society has shown an ambivalent attitude to many of these problems and yet seems to expect schools to overcome them. Nevertheless, the increasing interest in health education in schools should enable many children to enjoy a healthier and better socially adjusted adult life.

CHAPTER XI

THE SCHOOL DENTAL SERVICE

As the year 1972 drew to a close preparations were underway for a survey on the dental health of a nationally representative sample of schoolchildren. The survey which has been commissioned by the Secretary of State for Health and Social Security should provide the profession with an accurate assessment of the dental condition of schoolchildren, together with other useful information—for example, whether they utilise the school dental service, the general dental service, or neither. The clinical examinations are to be carried out by school dental officers.

Although available treatment statistics show a continuing improvement in the dental health of schoolchildren, the level of dental disease in children has always been greater than the ability of the service to contain or control it. The most effective preventive measure available is fluoridation of the public water supply but, regrettably, the number of Authorities who have adopted this safe measure has not altered sufficiently for any great measure of success in reducing caries to be reported. There has been a further increase in the number of dentists within the service which is now larger than ever. The number of young graduates recruited is particularly welcome and has had a rejuvinating effect. The standard of premises is almost uniformly high and a wide range of service is offered.

The Department's dental advisers have played their own part in assisting Authorities in their quest for higher standards and their routine visits were followed by written communication of both commendation and criticism, but leaving no doubts in the mind of the recipients of the Department's continued interest and willingness to be of assistance. The interchange of views between the officers in the field and Departmental Officers has been of advantage to both and an important factor in the improving standards within the service.

Whilst a degree of satisfaction is reasonable it must not mask the fact that almost all children suffer from dental disease and less than 20% receive an annual course of treatment within the school dental service. The biggest provider of treatment for children is the general dental service, which carried out over 6,000,000 courses last year for children of school age. The vulnerability of children to dental disease is well known and no one branch of the service can deal with the situation in a satisfactory manner. The increasing ability of the general dental service to offer comprehensive treatment to children has not affected the numbers of those wishing to utilise the school service, although it has played its part in producing a superior pattern of treatment.

The changes contemplated in reorganising the National Health Service and the integration of the school dental service within it, does not alter the basic premise that too many children suffer from dental disease and the need for children's dentistry will continue to be very great in the foreseeable future. There is every reason to believe that the momentum of improvement in the provision of dental services will continue after reorganisation and that the same sensitive and valuable relationship with schools will be maintained.

Staffing

The full-time equivalent of dentists working in the local authority service in England was 1,437 in 1972. This figure included a full-time equivalent of 84 dentists caring for children under school age and expectant and nursing mothers. The 713 part time dental officers within the service are a vital addition to salaried staff. Some part-time officers are general practitioners seeking an occasional change of environment for a variety of reasons, others are married women who might otherwise be lost to children's dentistry if employment was not available on a part-time basis.

Type of Treatment

Although the increase in the number of children treated in the past 20 years has been small the pattern of treatment has greatly improved. The brief visit for an extraction to relieve pain is much less common than hitherto. More fillings were inserted and more teeth preserved than ever before and there were fewer general anaesthetics. Treating the modern child is often more time consuming than in the past and whilst it is a cause for satisfaction that the child is receiving better dental treatment, it does indicate that the dental problems of the modern child will require more sophisticated dentistry as time passes and this factor underlines the need for effective preventive measures.

Dental Auxiliaries

The need for dental ancillaries is now so apparent that it is of interest to recall that the introduction of the dental auxiliary in 1958 was a controversial issue. The impact of the 218 Dental Auxiliaries working in England can be observed in the revised statistical returns which separate their work from that of dental officers. They provided treatment for 81,000 pupils, 51,000 of which were nine years of age or under and conserved 282,000 teeth by fillings. This by any standard was a major contribution to the dental health of children. There are but few dental hygienists within the service but their work on prophylaxis and dental health education makes a most valuable contribution.

Emergencies in Dental Practice

A booklet prepared by the Standing Dental Advisory Committee was distributed to dentists in all local authorities in November 1972. Drugs used in medical treatment such as corticosteroids, anti-coagulants, oral hypoglycaemic drugs, insulin, hypnotics or sedatives, antibiotics and antidepressants were considered as possible causes of emergency in the dental surgery and the precautions to be taken and the treatment administered is covered briefly, but satisfactorily, in the booklet.

Health Education

The need for effective dental education is great, but results are often disappointing or the success is transitory. It is a likely supposition that the dentists and ancillary workers within the school service are just too few in numbers to make much impact on 8,000,000 schoolchildren, yet attitudes have changed with time. There is now a genuine and growing desire for conservation. The mother is upset at the premature loss of her child's tooth and it may be that the parameters for measuring the success of the different programmes in the past have failed to register improvement due to their lack of sensitivity.

15,000 dental health education sessions were carried out by dentists and ancillary workers but more emphasis could be placed on providing information of interest for the class teacher for it is their expertise that gives them a key rôle in this field. Failure to recognise the importance of their rôle diminishes the potential for good in this important field.

APPENDIX A

STATISTICS OF THE SCHOOL HEALTH SERVICE

TABLE I

STAFF OF THE SCHOOL HEALTH SERVICE

	Medical Officers											Nurses and Health Visitors					
	Solely school health service		Part-time school health service/rest of time local health service		Part-time school health service/rest of time as general practitioner	Part-time school health service/rest of time on other medical work	Ophthalmic specialists		Other consultants and specialists		With health visitors' certificate		Without health visitors' certificate		Nurses' assistants	
	f.t.	p.t.	f.t.	p.t.	p.t.	p.t.	f.t.	p.t.	f.t.	p.t.	f.t.	p.t.	f.t.	p.t.	f.t.	p.t.
Number:																
1971 England	115	78	984	753	767	425	2	287	—	219	3,834	2,533	1,400	1,365	263	409
Wales	7	—	117	45	26	17	—	16	—	10	454	50	132	90	18	12
Total	122	78	1,101	798	793	442	2	303	—	229	4,288	2,583	1,532	1,455	281	421
Number:																
1972 England	121	84	1,099	661	802	443	5	320	1	231	4,058	2,392	1,282	1,460	302	406
Wales	3	1	112	47	25	35	—	17	—	13	450	68	164	112	15	13
Total	124	85	1,211	708	827	478	5	337	1	244	4,508	2,460	1,446	1,572	317	419
Whole-time equivalent:																
1971 England	142·2	4·4	706·2	59·0	92·5	66·8	61·5	2·2	20·7	1·1	1,760·7	187·7	1,634·9	60·4	339·3	13·9
Wales					2·8	4·5										
Total	146·6		765·2		95·3	71·3	63·7		21·8		1,948·4		1,695·3		353·2	
Whole-time equivalent:																
1972 England	142·7	3·1	684·8	63·1	87·5	67·8	65·3	2·4	23·5	1·5	1,666·3	108·7	1,501·9	94·4	354·5	11·2
Wales					4·3	9·6										
Total	145·8		747·9		91·8	77·4	67·7		25·0		1,775·0		1,596·3		365·7	

TABLE I—continued

STAFF OF THE SCHOOL HEALTH SERVICE

| | Speech Therapists | | | | | | Audio-metricians | | Chiropodists | | Orthoptists | | Physio-therapists | | Others (excluding clerical staff) | |
| | Senior speech therapists | | Speech therapists | | Assistant speech therapists | | | | | | | | | | | |
	f.t.	p.t.	f.t.	p.t.	f.t.	p.t.	f.t.	p.t.	f.t.	p.t.	f.t.	p.t.	f.t.	p.t.	f.t.	p.t.
Number:																
1971 England	77	30	319	413	1	1	75	87	53	157	10	48	150	203	130	100
Wales	3	2	10	18	–	1	3	6	–	2	–	3	2	9	1	–
Total	80	32	329	431	1	2	78	93	53	159	10	51	152	212	131	100
Number:																
1972 England	101	27	311	447	1	1	80	86	48	180	14	46	153	260	145	111
Wales	6	2	9	20	–	1	3	24	15	2	–	4	1	6	7	1
Total	107	29	320	467	1	2	83	110	63	182	14	50	154	266	152	112
Whole-time equivalent:																
1971 England	92·1	3·6	441·7	16·9	1·8	0·9	112·7	5·7	34·0	0·3	28·3	1·2	208·6	3·9	172·1	1·0
Total	95·7		458·6		2·7		118·4		34·3		29·5		212·5		173·1	
Whole-time equivalent:																
1972 England	117·9	5·7	472·6	18·1	1·4	0·8	117·0	5·7	34·0	1·0	25·6	1·4	234·4	2·5	190·2	7·3
Total	123·6		490·7		2·2		122·7		35·0		27·0		236·9		197·5	

TABLE II

Staff of the School Health Service—Child Guidance and School Psychological Service

	Psychiatrists				Educational Psychologists		Social Workers				Psycho-therapists		Remedial Teachers		Others (excluding Clerical Staff)	
	Employed by the local education authority		Employed under arrangements with hospital authority		Employed in Child Guidance Clinics	Employed in the School Psychological Service	Qualified		Unqualified							
	f.t.	p.t.	f.t.	p.t.			f.t.	p.t.	f.t.	p.t.	f.t.	p.t.	f.t.	p.t.	f.t.	p.t.
Number:																
1971 England	18	84	13	232		569	284	191	26	25	29	77	367	560	51	28
Wales	1	3	1	25		38	19	8	5	6	—	2	133	87	38	2
Total	19	87	14	257		607	303	199	31	31	29	79	500	647	89	30
Number:																
1972 England	22	84	19	251		650	244	163	43	35	32	82	435	595	88	42
Wales	—	5	3	20		44	19	9	3	2	—	—	80	35	1	2
Total	22	89	22	271		694	263	172	46	37	32	82	515	630	89	44
Whole-time equivalent:																
1971 England	42·3	1·8	95·5	8·2	206·9	316·8	365·0	20·0	40·1	5·1	53·8	0·5	553·6	176·7	63·3	39·0
Wales					5·3	25·7										
Total	44·1		103·7		212·2	342·5	385·0		45·2		54·3		730·3		102·3	
Whole-time equivalent:																
1972 England	46·8	1·4	107·0	7·1	230·3	372·9	353·5	22·4	58·1	4·0	64·5	—	681·6	100·5	108·9	2·0
Wales					6·5	28·7										
Total	48·2		114·1		236·8	401·6	375·9		62·1		64·5		782·1		110·9	

TABLE III

Medical Inspections

	Number of pupils on the registers of maintained and assisted primary secondary schools (including nursery and special schools) in January 1973	Number of pupils inspected during the year ended 31 December 1972	
		At periodic inspections	At special and re-inspections
England	8,165,946	1,543,661	1,123,113
Wales	520,502	87,835	53,535
Total	8,686,448	1,631,496	1,176,648

TABLE IV

NUMBER OF CERTAIN DEFECTS TO HAVE RECEIVED TREATMENT BY THE AUTHORITY OR OTHERWISE, HOWEVER THEY WERE BROUGHT TO LOCAL EDUCATION AUTHORITIES' NOTICE, I.E. WHETHER BY PERIODIC INSPECTION, SPECIAL INSPECTION OR OTHERWISE, DURING 1972

	Number of defects treated, or under treatment during the year 1972		
	England	Wales	Total
DISEASES OF THE SKIN:			
Ringworm—scalp	324	6	330
Ringworm—body	496	14	510
Scabies	12,010	371	12,381
Impetigo	7,248	126	7,374
Other skin diseases	133,355	2,243	135,598
EYE DISEASES: DEFECTIVE VISION AND SQUINT:			
External and other (excluding errors of refraction and squint)	25,199	2,931	28,130
Errors of refraction and squint	359,315	20,917	380,232
Number of pupils for whom spectacles were prescribed	179,013	10,280	189,293
DEFECTS OF EAR:			
Total number of pupils still on registers of school at 31 December known to have been provided with hearing aids:—			
a. during the calendar year	2,382	150	2,532
b. in previous year	13,773	705	14,478
CONVALESCENT TREATMENT:			
Number of pupils who received convalescent treatment under School Health Service arrangements	5,843	2	5,845
MINOR AILMENTS:			
Number of pupils with minor ailments	288,768	2,311	291,079

TABLE V

NUMBER OF CHILDREN KNOWN TO HAVE RECEIVED TREATMENT
UNDER CHILD GUIDANCE ARRANGEMENTS DURING THE YEAR
1972

		Number of clinics		Number of pupils treated	
		1971	1972	1971	1972
England	..	446	464	65,762	70,958
Wales	..	37	34	3,494	3,738
Total	..	483	498	69,256	74,696

TABLE VI

NUMBER OF CHILDREN KNOWN TO HAVE RECEIVED TREATMENT
UNDER SPEECH THERAPY ARRANGEMENTS DURING THE YEAR
1972

		Number of clinics		Number of pupils treated	
		1971	1972	1971	1972
England	..	1,502	1,448	90,557	99,407
Wales	..	116	124	3,888	4,502
Total	..	1,618	1,572	94,445	103,909

TABLE VII

UNCLEANLINESS AND VERMINOUS CONDITIONS FOUND DURING THE YEAR 1972

| | Total number of examinations of pupils in schools by school nurses or other authorised persons | | Total number of individual pupils found to be infested | | Number of individual pupils in respect of whom were issued | | | |
| | | | | | Cleansing Notices under Section 54(2) of the Education Act 1944 | | Cleansing Orders under Section 54(3) of the Education Act 1944 | |
	1971	1972	1971	1972	1971	1972	1971	1972
England	11,499,254	12,121,314	242,851	249,971	51,674	51,816	5,077	5,887
Wales	813,287	773,710	17,907	16,631	3,594	3,524	52	23
Total	12,312,541	12,895,024	260,758	266,602	55,268	55,340	5,129	5,910

TABLE VIII

Causes of death	Under 5 years of age		5–14 years of age		Total		Total male and female
	M	F	M	F	M	F	
1. Enteritis and other diarrhoeal diseases ..	242	168	5	1	247	169	416
2. Tuberculosis of respiratory system	—	1	—	—	—	1	1
3. Other tuberculosis, including late effects ..	3	4	—	4	3	8	11
4. Diphtheria ..	—	—	—	—	—	—	—
5. Whooping cough ..	1	1	—	—	1	1	2
6. Meningococcal infection ..	54	28	6	7	60	35	95
7. Acute poliomyelitis	—	—	—	—	—	—	—
8. Measles	7	11	4	5	11	16	27
9. Syphilis and its sequelae	—	—	—	—	—	—	—
10. All other infective and parasitic diseases	79	82	11	12	90	84	184
11. Malignant neoplasms of the stomach ..	1	—	—	—	1	—	1
12. Trachea, bronchus and lung ..	—	—	—	—	—	—	—
13. Breast	—	—	—	—	—	—	—
14. Cervix uteri and other uterus ..	—	—	—	1	—	1	1
15. Leukaemia, aleukaemia ..	68	55	120	84	188	139	327
16. Other malignant neoplasms ..	99	85	169	79	268	164	432
17. Diabetes mellitus	3	4	7	13	10	17	27
18. Hypertensive disease	—	1	—	—	—	1	1
19. Ischaemic heart disease	—	—	1	1	1	1	2
20. Other forms of heart disease ..	33	34	21	22	54	56	110
21. Cerebrovascular disease	15	6	25	15	40	21	61
22. Other circulatory diseases ..	9	6	3	1	12	7	19
23. Influenza	8	16	5	9	13	25	38
24. Pneumonia ..	753	567	61	57	814	624	1,438
25. Bronchitis, all forms	419	260	21	12	440	272	712
26. Other diseases of respiratory system	188	122	38	25	226	147	373
27. Peptic ulcer ..	1	2	2	—	3	2	5
28. Other diseases of digestive system	178	124	29	22	207	146	353
29. Nephritis and nephrosis ..	8	8	9	17	17	25	42

TABLE VIII—*continued*

Causes of death	Under 5 years of age		5–14 years of age		Total		Total male and female
	M	F	M	F	M	F	
30. Hyperplasia of prostate ..	—	—	—	—	—	—	—
31. Complications of pregnancy, child-birth and the puerperium ..	—	—	—	—	—	—	—
32. Congenital anomalies ..	1,588	1,549	117	121	1,705	1,670	3,375
33. Other defined and ill-defined diseases	4,124	2,794	193	160	4,317	2,954	7,271
34. Motor vehicle accidents ..	120	83	386	193	506	276	782
35. All other accidents	391	302	284	68	675	370	1,045
36. Suicide and self-inflicted injuries	—	—	5	—	5	—	5
37. All other external causes	53	48	18	17	71	65	136
All causes	8,445	6,361	1,540	946	9,985	7,307	17,292

TABLE IX

NET EXPENDITURE OF LOCAL EDUCATION
AUTHORITIES ON THE SCHOOL HEALTH SERVICE
FOR THE FINANCIAL YEAR 1971–72

	Net expenditure to be met from grants and rates (excluding loan charges, capital expenditure from revenue and capital expenditure from loans) (£000)
England	30,691
Wales	2,030
Total	32,721

TABLE X

NUMBERS OF CORRECTED NOTIFICATIONS OF INFECTIOUS DISEASES AMONG CHILDREN UNDER 15 DURING THE YEAR ENDED 31 DECEMBER 1972

ENGLAND AND WALES

| | Scarlet Fever | | Whooping Cough | | Acute Poliomyelitis | | | | Measles | | Diphtheria | | Dysentery | |
| | | | | | Paralytic | | Non-paralytic | | | | | | | |
	M	F	M	F	M	F	M	F	M	F	M	F	M	F
Under 5 years ..	1,764	1,558	649	672	—	—	—	—	39,419	37,375	1	—	1,732	1,510
5–14 years ..	3,487	3,632	324	364	1	—	1	1	34,043	32,158	1	1	1,270	1,011
Total	5,251	5,190	973	1,036	1	—	1	1	73,462	69,533	2	1	3,002	2,521

| | Smallpox | | Acute Encephalitis | | | | Enteric or typhoid fever | | Paratyphoid fever | | Tuberculosis (all forms) | | Acute meningitis | | Food poisoning | |
| | | | Infective | | Post-infectious | | | | | | | | | | | |
	M	F	M	F	M	F	M	F	M	F	M	F	M	F	M	F
Under 5 years ..	—	—	11	6	11	11	8	10	4	6	173	208	349	263	596	475
5–14 years ..	1	—	13	4	29	15	17	12	6	9	394	397	303	167	468	401
Total ..	1	—	24	10	40	26	25	22	10	15	567	605	652	430	1,064	876

NOTE: Acute pneumonia ceased to be notifiable on 23 September 1968.

63

APPENDIX B

STATISTICS OF THE SCHOOL DENTAL SERVICE

TABLE I

Staff of the School Dental Service as at 31 December

	Dental* Officers		Dental* Auxiliaries		Dental Surgery Assistants		Dental* Hygienists		Dental Technicians		Dental Health Education Personnel		Clerical Assistants	
	1971	1972	1971	1972	1971	1972	1971	1972	1971	1972	1971	1972	1971	1972
Number:														
England	1838	1846	200	218	1988	2137	17	19	106	105	23	27	164	152
Wales	125	121	15	15	141	143	—	—	4	4	4	4	2	2
Total	1963	1967	215	233	2129	2280	17	19	110	109	27	31	166	154
Whole-time Equivalent:														
England	1324·3	1353·1	150·4	174·2	1736·4	1608·9	10·7	11·3	101·7	99·7	12·5	13·2	113·1	118·9
Wales	97·0	96·8	14·2	14·3	119·3	121·8	—	—	4·0	4·0	2·2	2·4	0·8	0·8
Total	1421·3	1449·9	164·6	188·5	1855·7	1730·7	10·7	11·3	105·7	103·7	14·7	15·6	113·9	119·7

* Excluding Maternity and Child Health

TABLE II

DENTAL INSPECTION AND TREATMENT DURING THE YEAR ENDED 31 DECEMBER

(A) NUMBER OF PUPILS

Number of pupils on registers in January, 1973 = 8,686,448 (England = 8,165,946; Wales = 520,502)

	First inspection			Number found to require treatment	Number offered treatment	Number actually treated	% age of pupils found to require treatment who received it	Number of pupils re-inspected at School or Clinic	Number of re-inspected pupils found to require treatment	Attendances made by pupils for treatment
	At school	At clinic	Total							
1971 England	3,806,830	719,030	4,525,860	2,508,218	2,191,885	1,295,064	51·6	433,732	258,279	3,525,734
Wales	192,259	52,816	245,075	158,998	143,515	89,693	56·4	19,669	12,878	234,016
Total	3,999,089	771,846	4,770,935	2,667,216	2,335,400	1,384,757	51·9	453,401	271,157	3,759,750
1972 England	3,965,718	758,561	4,724,279	2,572,713	2,245,780	1,342,515	52·2	441,383	259,256	3,639,500
Wales	184,038	53,813	237,851	146,576	139,422	88,100	60·1	20,560	13,538	236,630
Total	4,149,756	812,374	4,962,130	2,719,289	2,385,202	1,430,615	52·6	461,943	272,794	3,876,130

TABLE II—continued

(B) DENTAL TREATMENT (OTHER THAN ORTHODONTIC TREATMENT—SEE TABLE II(C))—DURING THE YEAR ENDED 31 DECEMBER

	Sessions devoted to			Number of fillings		Number of teeth filled		Number of extractions		Teeth otherwise conserved
	Treatment	Inspection	Dental health education	Permanent teeth	Deciduous teeth	Permanent teeth	Deciduous teeth	Permanent teeth	Deciduous teeth	
1969 England	555,749	33,576	15,055	2,176,423	984,355	1,831,677	877,831	273,280	800,138	150,727
Wales	40,830	1,863	1,207	138,059	55,999	113,495	49,024	25,987	59,617	14,537
Total	596,579	35,439	16,262	2,314,482	1,040,354	1,945,172	926,855	299,267	859,755	165,264
1972 England	567,939	37,782	14,571	2,207,230	1,024,291	1,859,427	913,783	285,128	806,181	153,571
Wales	41,276	2,052	849	142,654	58,192	117,698	50,390	24,596	55,194	16,233
Total	609,215	39,834	15,420	2,349,884	1,082,483	1,977,125	964,173	309,724	861,375	169,804

	Crowns	Inlays	Teeth root filled	Dentures		Number of pupils X-rayed		Number of general anaesthetics administered by	
				Number of pupils supplied with dentures	Number of dentures supplied		Prophylaxis	Dental Officers	Medical Practitioners
1971 England	7,278	734	9,822	5,688	6,930	108,615	372,265	85,898	237,069
Wales	572	64	753	504	577	4,098	24,996	6,929	24,186
Total	7,850	798	10,575	6,192	7,507	112,713	397,261	92,827	261,255
1972 England	7,663	780	10,044	5,972	7,329	120,707	397,162	80,788	229,881
Wales	806	48	846	569	648	4,689	24,602	3,912	21,639
Total	8,469	828	10,890	6,541	7,977	125,396	421,764	84,700	251,520

TABLE II—continued

(C) Orthodontic Treatment during the year ended 31 December

	Number of cases			Number of appliances fitted		Number of pupils referred to Hospital Consultants
	Commenced during the year	Completed during the year	Discontinued during the year	Removable	Fixed	
1971 England :: ::	22,344	16,766	3,090	37,923	2,485	4,641
Wales :: ::	1,355	752	160	1,285	329	558
Total :: ::	23,699	17,518	3,250	39,208	2,814	5,199
1972 England :: ::	24,082	18,138	3,143	39,972	2,419	5,131
Wales :: ::	1,381	643	85	1,585	310	799
Total :: ::	25,463	18,781	3,228	41,557	2,729	5,930

TABLE III

DENTAL ATTENDANCES AND TREATMENT BY AGE GROUPS DURING THE YEAR ENDED 31 DECEMBER 1972

	Ages 5–9		Ages 10–14		Ages 15 and over		Total		Total England and Wales
	England	Wales	England	Wales	England	Wales	England	Wales	
Number of first visits (i.e. pupils treated)	674,605	45,121	555,511	35,003	112,399	7,976	1,342,515	88,100	1,430,615
Subsequent visits	938,639	63,230	1,112,293	67,403	246,053	17,897	2,296,985	148,530	2,445,515
Total visits	1,613,244	108,351	1,667,804	102,406	358,452	25,873	3,639,500	236,630	3,876,130
Additional courses of treatment commenced	85,933	3,091	68,307	2,472	14,069	648	168,309	6,211	174,520
Fillings in permanent teeth	573,337	34,002	1,281,059	81,208	352,834	27,444	2,207,230	142,654	2,349,884
Fillings in deciduous teeth	923,965	52,811	100,326	5,381			1,024,291	58,192	1,082,483
Permanent teeth filled	459,121	27,002	1,092,372	68,278	307,934	22,418	1,859,427	117,698	1,977,125
Deciduous teeth filled	824,496	45,890	89,287	4,500			913,783	50,390	964,173
Permanent teeth extracted	46,356	3,961	196,896	15,909	41,876	4,726	285,128	24,596	309,724
Deciduous teeth extracted	602,019	42,136	204,162	13,058			806,181	55,194	861,375
General anaesthetics	195,467	15,779	104,048	8,552	11,154	1,220	310,669	25,551	336,220
Emergencies (treatment)	100,250	7,458	61,646	4,089	11,602	950	173,498	12,497	185,995
Courses of treatment completed	—	—	—	—	—	—	1,200,268	70,847	1,271,115

TABLE IV

PROSTHETICS 1972 (BY AGE GROUPS)

		Ages 5–9	Ages 10–14	Ages 15 and over	Total
Pupils fitted with full dentures for the first time	England	18	75	152	245
	Wales	2	9	43	54
	Total	20	84	195	299
Pupils supplied with other dentures for the first time	England	411	3,464	1,852	5,727
	Wales	19	268	228	515
	Total	430	3,732	2,080	6,242
Number of dentures supplied (first or subsequent time)	England	497	4,248	2,584	7,329
	Wales	21	311	316	648
	Total	518	4,559	2,900	7,977

69

TABLE V

ANALYSIS OF DUTIES OF DENTAL OFFICERS, DENTAL AUXILIARIES AND DENTAL HYGIENISTS FOR THE YEAR ENDED 31 DECEMBER ENGLAND AND WALES

i. Dental Officers

	Number of Officers		Total full-time equivalent inclusive of extra paid sessions work					
			Administrative duties		Clinical duties			
					School Service		M & CH Service	
	1971	1972	1971	1972	1971	1972	1971	1972
PSDO	175	174	67·0	67·0	98·8	96·8	9·6	10·6
Dental Officers (employed on salary basis)	1129	1159	15·2	17·9	1034·1	1065·1	65·5	65·4
Dental Officers (employed on sessional basis)	659	634	—	—	206·2	203·1	15·2	13·7
Total	1963	1967	82·2	84·9	1339·1	1365·0	90·3	89·7

ii. Dental Auxiliaries and Dental Hygienists

| | Number of Officers | | Full-time equivalent | | | |
| | | | School Service | | M & CH Service | |
	1971	1972	1971	1972	1971	1972
Dental Hygienists	17	19	10·7	11·3	0·6	1·7
Dental Auxiliaries	215	233	164·6	188·5	35·5	16·5

APPENDIX C

HANDICAPPED PUPILS REQUIRING AND RECEIVING EDUCATION IN SPECIAL SCHOOLS APPROVED UNDER SECTION 9(5) OF THE EDUCATION ACT, 1944: RECEIVING EDUCATION IN INDEPENDENT SCHOOLS, IN SPECIAL CLASSES AND UNITS; BOARDED IN HOMES AND RECEIVING EDUCATION IN ACCORDANCE WITH SECTION 56 OF THE EDUCATION ACT

ENGLAND AND WALES

	Blind	Partially sighted	Deaf	Partially hearing	Physically handi-capped	Delicate	Mal-adjusted	ESN	Epileptic	Suffering from Speech defects	Total
1. During the year ending 31 December 1971, number of handicapped pupils who were:											
A. Newly assessed as needing special educational treatment at special schools or in boarding homes	160	371	356	624	1,974	2,186	3,648	14,311	341	147	24,148
B. Newly placed in special schools (other than hospital special schools) or boarding homes	143	304	321	545	1,764	1,964	2,883	13,286	169	111	21,490
2. In January, 1972 number of handicapped children who were:											
A. Requiring places in special schools (i) Day	8	86	55	149	488	288	297	9,431	5	36	10,843
(ii) Boarding	119	130	72	88	245	550	1,525	1,797	44	74	4,644
B. On the registers of maintained special schools (i) Day	34	1,225	1,530	1,505	6,809	3,983	2,654	73,157	244	351	91,073
(ii) Boarding	230	427	419	376	1,224	1,955	2,639	7,886	119	19	15,294
C. On the registers of non-maintained special schools (i) Day	34	55	196	75	333	5	3	273	—	5	979
(ii) Boarding	806	400	1,263	466	1,181	661	1,020	1,210	461	82	7,550
D. On the registers of independent schools under arrangements made by local education authorities	5	17	240	130	651	186	3,257	1,000	8	27	5,520
E. Boarded in Homes and not already included in 2B, C or D above	1		4	1	10	90	669	50	1	—	826
F. Being educated under arrangements made in accordance with Section 56 of the Education Act, 1944 (i) in hospitals	1	1	9	2	362	247	344	288	7	3	1,264
(ii) in other groups	5	5	2	36	526	34	972	439	14	6	2,037
(iii) at home	10	19	9	13	831	287	517	309	37	7	2,039
G. Being educated in special classes or units not forming part of special schools		75		2,559	212	168	2,133				5,147
Total receiving special educational treatment and awaiting places	1,253	2,439	3,799	4,981	12,872	8,452	16,030	95,840	940	610	147,216

(a) On 1 April 1971, local education authorities became responsible for 28,085 children who had previously been regarded as unsuitable for education at school. These children are included in the above table.

(b) In January 1972, 8,626 pupils were on the registers of hospital special schools but not included in the above table.

APPENDIX D

MEDICAL AND DENTAL STAFFS OF THE DEPARTMENT OF EDUCATION AND SCIENCE 1971/1972

Medical Officers

Chief Medical Officer*
Sir George Godber, G.C.B., D.M., F.R.C.P., D.P.H.

Senior Principal Medical Officer
Dr. E. E. Simpson, M.D., B.S., F.R.C.P., F.F.C.M., D.P.H., D.C.H.

Senior Medical Officers
Dr. T. K. Whitmore, M.R.C.S., L.R.C.P., D.C.H.
Dr. M. Scott Stevenson, M.B., Ch.B., M.F.C.M., D.P.H.

Medical Officers
Dr. R. Burns, L.R.C.P., L.R.C.S., L.R.F.P.S.
Dr. J. L. Evans, M.B., B.S., M.R.C.S., L.R.C.P., D.P.H., D.Obst.R.C.O.G.
Dr. S. R. Fine, M.B., Ch.B., M.F.C.M., D.P.H., D.C.H., Barrister-at-Law
Dr. M. L. Graeme, V.R.D., M.A., M.B., B.Chir., M.F.C.M., M.R.C.S., L.R.C.P., D.P.H.
Dr. N. P. Halliday, M.B., B.S., M.R.C.S., L.R.C.P., D.C.H.
Dr. M. B. Pepper, M.B., B.S., D.P.H.
†Dr. F. M. Richards, B.Sc., M.B., B.Ch., D.Obst.R.C.O.G., D.P.H., D.C.H.
Dr. E. Wales, M.B., B.S., D.P.H., D.C.H., D.Obst.R.C.O.G.

Dental Officers

Chief Dental Officer*
G. D. Gibb, L.D.S., R.C.S.

Senior Dental Officer*
J. Rodgers, D.F.M., L.D.S., R.F.P.S.

Dental Officers
J. G. Potter, L.D.S., R.F.P.S.
W. G. Everett, L.D.S., D.D.P.H., R.C.S.
C. Howard, B.D.S., L.D.S., D.D.P.H., R.C.S.

* These officers are jointly employed by the Department of Health and Social Security and the Department of Education and Science

† This officer is jointly employed by the Welsh Office and the Department of Education and Science

SCHOOL HEALTH AND DENTAL SERVICES

TABLE SHOWING THE NAMES OF THE PRINCIPAL SCHOOL MEDICAL OFFICERS EMPLOYED BY EACH LOCAL EDUCATION AUTHORITY, TOGETHER WITH THE NUMBER OF PUPILS ON REGISTERS OF MAINTAINED AND ASSISTED PRIMARY AND SECONDARY (INCLUDING NURSERY AND SPECIAL SCHOOLS) IN JANUARY 1973.

ENGLAND (COUNTIES)

Local Education Authority	Name of Principal School Medical Officer	Name of Principal School Dental Officer	No. of Pupils on Registers January 1973
Bedfordshire	M. C. Macleod ..	H. W. S. Sheasby ..	55,637
Berkshire	D. E. Cullington ..	G. Ogilvy	95,807
Buckinghamshire ..	J. J. A. Reid	C. H. Griffiths ..	111,932
Cambridgeshire and Isle of Ely	M. E. Hocken	J. C. McIntyre ..	49,852

Local Education Authority	Name of Principal School Medical Officer	Name of Principal School Dental Officer	No. of Pupils on Registers January 1973
Cheshire	B. G. Gretton-Watson	T. B. Dowell	205,642
Cornwall	H. Binysh	L. Jones	62,453
Cumberland	J. Leiper	R. B. Neal	42,057
Derbyshire	A. H. Snaith	H. E. Gray	116,986
Devon	J. Lyons	F. H. Stewart	67,541
Dorset	G. F. Willson	J. S. MacLachlan	58,325
Durham	S. Ludkin	Mrs. M. M. Lishman	157,447
Essex	J. A. C. Franklin	J. C. Timmis	220,645
Gloucestershire	A. Withnell	J. F. A. Smith	105,212
Hampshire	I. A. MacDougall	M. V. Symes	184,177
Herefordshire	P. J. C. Walker	O. S. Bennett	24,257
Hertfordshire	G. W. Knight	A. H. Millett	181,094
Huntingdon and Peterborough	G. Nisbet	I. O. Pinkham	41,576
Isle of Wight	R. K. Machell	W. Maden	16,904
Isles of Scilly	C. M. Mills	B. I. Fairest	317
Kent	A. Elliott	E. Millward	237,248
Lancashire	C. H. T. Wade	G. Entwisle	466,808
Leicestershire	A. R. Buchan	G. A. Scivier	89,466
LincolnshireHolland	J. Fielding	K. Jackson	18,242
Lincolnshire Kesteven	E. W. Birch	J. E. Mann	28,742
Lincolnshire Lindsey	C. D. Cormac	J. Watson	73,005
Norfolk	A. G. Scott	N. J. Rowland	75,555
Northamptonshire	W. J. McQuillan	P. W. Gibson	64,683
Northumberland	J. B. Tilley	C. L. Carmichael	90,691
Nottinghamshire	H. I. Lockett	K. H. Davis	125,073
Oxfordshire	M. J. Pleydell	T. Lucas	49,868
Rutland	R. A. Matthews	Miss J. G. Campbell	5,104
Salop	P. Moore	C. D. Clarke	62,217
Somerset	A. Parry-Jones	J. D. Palmer	100,708
Staffordshire	G. Ramage	W. McKay	139,264
Suffolk East	S. T. G. Gray	C. D. Macpherson	39,436
Suffolk West	D. G. H. Patey	E. Ferguson	29,636
Surrey	J. Drummond	O. H. Minton	156,573
Sussex East	J. A. G. Watson	C. K. Fenton Evans	63,210
Sussex West	T. McL. Galloway	P. S. R. Conron	78,035
Warwickshire	G. H. Taylor	H. J. Bastow	120,769
Westmorland	H. P. Ferrar	M. D. McGarry	12,252
Wiltshire	C. D. L. Lycett	D. M. Middleton	92,691
Worcestershire	J. D. Willins	C. W. D. Jones	78,556
Yorks, East Riding	W. Ferguson	G. R. Smith	44,526
Yorks, North Riding	J. T. A. George	Miss A. Potts	54,911
Yorks, West Riding	R. W. Elliott	H. Taylor	332,747

ENGLAND (COUNTY BOROUGHS)

Barnsley	G. A. W. Neill	G. White	15,484
Barrow-in-Furness	A. W. Hay	D. J. Harrison	12,178
Bath	R. M. Ross	G. G. Davis	12,674
Birkenhead	P. O. Nicholas	W. M. Shaw	24,922
Birmingham	E. L. M. Millar	F. J. Hastilow	194,398
Blackburn	J. Ardley	J. Rigby	19,926
Blackpool	D. W. Wauchob	H. Gleek	21,393
Bolton	A. I. Ross	S. M. Aalen	29,470
Bootle	G. T. MacCulloch	D. W. Maxfield	15,595
Bournemouth	R. H. Browning	Mrs. M. B. Redfern	19,136
Bradford	W. Turner	M. J. M. Mackay	57,915
Brighton	W. S. Parker	J. B. Herington	22,984
Bristol	R. C. Wofinden	J. McCaig	71,709

Local Education Authority	Name of Principal School Medical Officer	Name of Principal School Dental Officer	No. of Pupils on Registers January 1973
Burnley ..	L. J. Collins ..	C. F. Tehan ..	15,795
Burton upon Trent	G. M. Curtois ..	A. N. Stannard	11,117
Bury ..	G. A. Levell ..	F. J. Heap ..	12,092
Canterbury	M. S. Harvey ..	A. G. L. Payne	6,124
Carlisle ..	D. G. Proudler ..	H. W. Freer ..	13,707
Chester ..	D. F. Morgan ..	G. H. Stout ..	11,884
Coventry	G. T. Pollock ..	J. A. Smith ..	67,312
Darlington	W. M. Markham	P. Waterfall ..	17,061
Derby ..	V. N. Leyshon ..	F. Grossman ..	40,899
Dewsbury	W. B. Whisker ..	T. Luxford ..	10,178
Doncaster	D. Randall-Martin	A. D. Anderson	16,567
Dudley ..	G. M. Reynolds	Mrs. J. P. McEwan	33,686
Eastbourne	K. A. O. Vickery	A. J. Lawrence	8,381
Exeter ..	G. P. McLauchlan	E. G. Reader ..	14,319
Gateshead	D. F. Henley ..	Miss T. M. Rossi	16,915
Gloucester	P. T. Regester ..	R. Bell ..	19,145
Great Yarmouth	R. G. Newberry	B. C. Clay ..	9,460
Grimsby	R. Glenn ..	G. S. Watson ..	19,785
Halifax ..	J. G. Cairns ..	W. E. Crosland	16,126
Hartlepool	H. C. Milligan	Mrs. K. M. Atkinson ..	20,762
Hastings	T. H. Parkman	Miss E. B. Nasmyth	10,430
Huddersfield	J. S. W. Brierley	J. A. E. Morris	23,126
Ipswich ..	B. A. Smith ..	K. J. Pratt ..	21,584
Kingston upon Hull	A. Hutchinson	C. D. Cox ..	56,362
Leeds ..	D. B. Bradshaw	J. Millar ..	89,115
Leicester	B. J. L. Moss ..	R. H. Bettles ..	56,200
Lincoln ..	R. D. Haigh ..	G. A. Vega ..	14,194
Liverpool	A. B. Semple ..	P. E. Goward ..	118,905
Luton ..	A. W. C. Lobban	J. W. Coombs ..	33,292
Manchester	K. Campbell ..	G. L. Lindley ..	101,346
Newcastle	D. L. Wilson ..	J. C. Brown ..	36,755
Northampton ..	W. Edgar ..	P. W. Gibson ..	24,035
Norwich	J. R. Murdock	P. I. Christensen	19,743
Nottingham	E. J. More ..	N. H. Whitehouse	57,371
Oldham	B. Gilbert ..	J. Fenton ..	20,230
Oxford ..	J. F. Warin ..	C. H. I. Millar ..	17,827
Plymouth	T. A. I. Rees ..	T. S. Longworth	41,919
Portsmouth	P. G. Roads ..	P. D. Bristow ..	30,024
Preston	J. T. Carroll ..	A. Kershaw ..	18,954
Reading	A. Gatherer ..	D. O. Mallam ..	23,682
Rochdale	R. G. Murray ..	H. W. Pritchard	18,877
Rotherham	I. F. Ralph ..	Miss J. H. Egan	16,788
St Helens	J. H. E. Baines	J. P. H. Donovan	20,630
Salford	D. J. Roberts ..	E. Rose ..	25,652
Sheffield	C. H. Shaw ..	E. Copestake ..	93,381
Solihull	I. M. McLachlan	E. F. Stonehouse	20,623
Southampton ..	A. McGregor ..	I. H. Maddick ..	38,536
Southend-on-Sea	G. V. Griffin ..	J. M. Stratford	25,963
Southport	P. W. Lang ..	W. L. Rothwell	13,928
South Shields ..	E. M. Young ..	T. W. Clarkson	18,708
Stockport	A. R. M. Moir ..	Miss F. Sellers ..	25,028
Stoke-on-Trent	J. S. Hamilton ..	G. T. Emery ..	47,758
Sunderland	A. Martin ..	F. J. Lishman ..	43,801
Teesside	R. J. Donaldson	R. S. Blackmore	87,152
Torbay ..	D. K. MacTaggart	G. J. Derbyshire	14,282
Tynemouth	G. MacA. Dowson	N. A. Eddy ..	13,605
Wakefield	D. B. Reynolds	R. E. Whittam ..	10,469
Wallasey	W. F. Christian	W. J. Meakin ..	17,693
Walsall	J. C. Talbot ..	Mrs. I. M. Millar ..	36,672
Warley	R. J. Dodds ..	J. Charlton ..	29,257
Warrington	G. Chandy ..	A. C. Crawford ..	13,627

Local Education Authority	Name of Principal School Medical Officer	Name of Principal School Dental Officer	No. of Pupils on Registers January 1973
West Bromwich ..	H. O. M. Bryant ..	J. B. C. Cuzner ..	31,740
Wigan	J. Haworth-Hilditch ..	N. Gleave ..	15,130
Wolverhampton ..	F. N. Garratt ..	S. Awath-Behari ..	52,770
Worcester ..	G. M. O'Donnell ..	K. Nicholas	13,620
York	S. R. W. Moore ..	G. Turner	18,967

LONDON

Authority	Name of Central Medical Adviser	Name of Central Dental Adviser	
Inner London	A. B. Stewart	K. C. B. Webster ..	

Authority	Name of Principal School Medical Officer	Name of Principal School Dental Officer	No. of Pupils on Registers January 1973
Inner London Boroughs			
Camden	W. G. Harding ..	G. P. Mailer	23,311
Greenwich	J. Kerr-Brown	F. Elston	41,589
Hackney	R. G. Davies	S. Gelbier	37,036
Hammersmith	A. D. C. S. Cameron ..	P. T. Fuller	27,130
Islington ..	C. Burns	R. Hyman	31,943
Royal Borough of Kensington & Chelsea	D. J. Sheerboom ..	A. Longden	15,185
Lambeth	A. L. Thrower	B. M. Spalding ..	48,121
Lewisham	A. W. Tranter	C. M. Leeming ..	46,591
Southwark	J. E. Epsom	J. J. Cleary	50,042
Tower Hamlets ..	R. W. Watton	T. H. H. Murray ..	30,506
Wandsworth	H. E. A. Carson ..	A. F. Weedon	49,650
City of Westminster ..	J. H. Briscoe-Smith ..	D. K. Hardy	21,303
City of London ..	W. G. Swann	L. J. Wallace	171
Outer London Boroughs			
Barking	J. Adrian Gillet ..	J. K. Whitelaw ..	28,903
Barnet	M. Watkins	R. L. James	47,390
Bexley	H. James	J. H. Forrester ..	37,802
Brent	C. Hollman	A. D. Henderson ..	44,974
Bromley	L. R. L. Edwards ..	Mrs C. M. Lindsey ..	48,202
Croydon	S. L. Wright	B. J. West	57,482
Ealing	I. H. Sheppelt	Miss K. M. F. Robinson	48,056
Enfield	W. D. Hyde	T. J. H. Phillips ..	44,335
Haringey	J. L. Patton	G. C. H. Kramer ..	40,658
Harrow	C. C. A. Jansz	A. G. Brown	31,936
Havering	F. Groake	E. B. Hodgson ..	46,529
Hillingdon	J. S. Horner	Mrs. B. Fox	40,883
Hounslow	R. L. Lindon	D. H. Norman ..	35,227
Kingston upon Thames	J. C. Birchall	D. M. Dodd	21,707
Merton	E. H. Todd	E. T. Thompson ..	26,862
Newham	N. S. Galbraith ..	P. Chandler	43,335
Redbridge	F. W. Murphy	E. V. Haigh	35,374
Richmond upon Thames	A. M. Nelson	G. H. Tucker	21,278
Sutton	W. H. K. Kinstrie ..	Mrs. B. M. Stewart ..	25,700
Waltham Forest ..	E. Walter Wright ..	R. Ward	36,870

WALES (COUNTIES)

Local Education Authority	Name of Principal School Medical Officer	Name of Principal School Dental Officer	No. of Pupils on Registers January 1973
Anglesey	G. Crompton	O. C. Jenkins	11,491
Breconshire	R. G. Evans	J. H. Sutcliffe	9,793
Caernarvonshire	C. T. Baynes	I. L. Williams	20,585
Cardiganshire	I. Morgan Watkin	W. D. Percival Evans	9,894
Carmarthenshire	G. Jones	S. C. R. Evans	27,348
Denbighshire	M. T. Islwyn Jones	D. R. Pearse	33,676
Flintshire	G. W. Roberts	A. Fielding	35,508
Glamorganshire	C. J. Revington	D. R. Edwards	146,697
Merioneth	E. Richards	W. B. Wolfe	6,306
Monmouthshire	A. J. Essex-Cater	E. F. Sumner	69,270
Montgomeryshire	E. S. Lovgreen	N. J. Riches	8,321
Pembrokeshire	D. J. Davies	D. G. James	19,809
Radnorshire	F. J. H. Crawford	D. M. Hobbs	3,277

WALES (COUNTY BOROUGHS)

Cardiff	D. J. W. Anderson	H. Newcombe	53,234
Merthyr Tydfil	R. M. Williams	F. S. Baguley	10,648
Newport	W. B. Clark	B. G. Hobby	23,579
Swansea	D. E. Donald	R. F. Hoar	31,066

Printed in England for Her Majesty's Stationery Office by McCorquodale Printers Ltd., London.
HM 6578. Dd. 506669. K 44. 3/74.